QUESTIONS AND ANSWERS
ABOUT ISLAM
VOL. 2

QUESTIONS & ANSWERS
about ISLAM
VOL. 2

M. Fethullah Gülen

Translated by Muhammed Çetin

TUGHRA
BOOKS

New Jersey

Published by Tughra Books
345 Clifton Ave., Clifton,
NJ, 07011, USA

www.tughrabooks.com
http://en.fgulen.com

Translated from Turkish by Muhammed Çetin

Library of Congress Cataloging-in-Publication Data

Gülen, Fethullah.
    [Asrin getirdiği tereddütler. English]
    Questions and answers about Islam / M. Fethullah Gülen.
      p. cm.
    Includes bibliographical references (p.   ) and index.
    ISBN 1-932099-25-5 (v. 2 : alk. paper)
      1. Islam--Theology--Miscellanea. 2. Islam--Doctrines--Miscellanea.   I. Title.
    BP166.G8513 2005
    297.2--dc22

                                                                    2005022436

ISBN 978-1-932099-25-6 (Paperback)
ISBN 978-1-59784-203-7 (Hardcover)

Printed by
Çağlayan A.Ş., Izmir / Turkey

TABLE OF CONTENTS

Chapter 1
WISDOM IN THE MESSAGE OF THE QUR'AN

Chapter 2
ETHICS AND SPIRITUALITY

Chapter 3
VIRTUES AND HARDSHIPS IN THE SERVICE OF ISLAM

ABOUT THE AUTHOR

Born in Erzurum, in eastern Turkey, in 1938, M. Fethullah Gülen is one of the world's most prominent and influential Islamic intellectuals.* He was trained in the religious sciences by several celebrated Muslim scholars and spiritual masters. Gülen also studied the principles and theories of modern social and physical sciences. Based on his exceptional skills in learning and focused self-study, he soon surpassed his peers. In 1959, after attaining excellent examination results, he was awarded a state preacher's license (in Edirne), and was promoted to a post in Izmir, Turkey's third largest province, in 1966. It was here that Gülen started to crystallize his theme and expand his audience base. In his sermons and speeches he emphasized the pressing social issues of the times: his particular aim was to urge the younger generation to harmonize intellectual enlightenment with wise spirituality and a caring, humane activism.

Gülen did not restrict himself to teaching in the inner cities. He traveled around the provinces in Anatolia and lectured not only in mosques, but also at town meetings and corner coffee houses. This enabled him to reach a more representative cross-section of the population and to attract the attention of the academic community, especially the student body. The subject matter of his speeches, whether formal or informal, was not restricted explicitly to religious questions; he also talked about education, science, Darwinism, about the economy and social justice. It was the depth and quality of his speeches on such a wide range of topics that most impressed the academic community, and won their attention and respect.

Questions and Answers About Islam Vol. 2

Gülen retired from formal teaching duties in 1981, having inspired a whole generation of young students. His efforts, dating from the 1960s, especially in educational reform, have made him one of the best-known and respected figures in Turkey. From 1988 to 1991, he gave a series of sermons as preacher emeritus in some of the most famous mosques in major population centers, while continuing to deliver his message in the form of popular conferences, not only in Turkey, but also in Western Europe.

MAIN IDEAS

In his speeches and writings Gülen envisions a twenty-first century in which we shall witness the birth of a spiritual dynamic that will revitalize long-dormant moral values; an age of tolerance, understanding, and international cooperation that will ultimately lead, through intercultural dialogue and a sharing of values, to a single, inclusive civilization. In the field of education, he has spearheaded the establishment of many charitable organizations to work for the welfare of the community, both within and without Turkey. He has inspired the use of mass media, notably television, to inform the public, of matters of pressing concern to them, individually and collectively.

Gülen believes the road to justice for all is dependent on the provision of an adequate and appropriate universal education. Only then will there be sufficient understanding and tolerance to secure respect for the rights of others. To this end, he has, over the years, encouraged the social elite and community leaders, powerful industrialists as well as small businessmen, to support quality education. With donations from these sources, educational trusts have been able to establish many schools, both in Turkey and abroad.

Gülen has stated that in the modern world the only way to get others to accept your ideas is by persuasion. He describes those who resort to force as being intellectually bankrupt; people will always demand freedom of choice in the way they run their affairs and in their expression of their spiritual and religious values. Democracy, Gülen argues, in spite of its many shortcomings, is now the only viable political system, and people should strive to modernize and consolidate democratic institutions in order to build a society where individual rights and freedoms are respected and protected, where equal opportunity for all is more than a dream.

INTERFAITH AND INTERCULTURAL ACTIVITIES

Since his retirement, Gülen has concentrated his efforts on establishing a dialogue among the factions representing different ideologies, cultures, religions and nations. In 1999, his paper "The Necessity of Interfaith Dialogue" was presented to the Parliament of World's Religions in Cape Town, December 1-8. He maintains that "dialogue is a must" and that people, regardless of nation or political borders, have far more in common than they realize.

Given all of this, Gülen considers it both worthwhile and necessary for a sincere dialogue to be established in order to increase mutual understanding. To this end, he has helped to establish the Journalists and Writers Foundation (1994), whose activities to promote dialogue and tolerance among all strata of the society have been warmly welcomed by people from almost all walks of life. Again to this end, Gülen visits and receives leading figures, not only from among the Turkish population, but from all over the world. Pope John Paul II at the Vatican, the late John O'Connor, Archbishop of New York, Leon Levy, former president of The Anti-Defamation League are among many leading representatives of world religions with whom Gülen has met to discuss dialogue and take initiatives in this respect. In Turkey, the Vatican's Ambassador to Turkey, the Patriarch of the Turkish Orthodox Church, the Patriarch of the Turkish Armenian community, the Chief Rabbi of the Turkish Jewish community and many other leading figures in Turkey have frequently met with him, portraying an example of how sincere dialogue can be established between people of faith.

In his meeting with Pope John Paul II at the Vatican (1998), Gülen presented a proposal to take firm steps to stop the conflict in the Middle East via collaborative work on this soil, a place where all three religions originated. In his proposal, he also underlined the fact that science and religion are in fact two different aspects that emanate from the same truth: "Humankind from time to time has denied religion in the name of science and denied science in the name of religion, arguing that the two present conflicting views. All knowledge belongs to God and religion is from God. How then can the two be in conflict? To this end, our joint efforts directed at inter-religious dialogue can do much to improve understanding and tolerance among people."

Gülen released a press declaration renouncing the September 11th terrorist attacks on the USA, which he regarded as a great blow to world peace that unfairly tarnished the credit of believers: ". . . terror can never be used in the name of Islam or for the sake of any Islamic ends. A terrorist cannot be a Muslim and a Muslim cannot be a terrorist. A Muslim can only be the representative and symbol of peace, welfare, and prosperity."

Gülen's efforts for worldwide peace have been echoed at conferences and symposiums. "The Peaceful Heroes Symposium" (April 11-13, 2003) at the University of Texas, Austin, produced a list of peacemakers over 5,000 years of human history. Gülen was mentioned among contemporary heroes of peace, in a list which includes names such as Jesus, Buddha, Mohandas Gandhi, Martin Luther King, Jr., and Mother Teresa.

In March 2004, the Spirituality Foundation of Kyrgyzstan awarded Gülen with its "Intersociety Adaptation and Contribution to Peace Prize" for his contribution to international peace through his thoughts and activities in education.

Gülen contributes to a number of journals and magazines. He writes the editorial page for several magazines. He writes the lead article for *The Fountain*, *Yeni Ümit*, *Sızıntı*, and *Yağmur*, leading popular and spiritual thought magazines in Turkey. He has written more than forty books, hundreds of articles, and recorded thousands of audio and videocassettes. He has delivered innumerable speeches on many social and religious issues. Some of his books—many of which have been best-sellers in Turkey—have been made available in English translations, such as, *The Messenger of God: Muhammad: An Analysis of the Prophet's Life, Toward a Global Civilization of Love and Tolerance, Questions and Answers about Faith, Pearls of Wisdom, The Essentials of the Islamic Faith, Towards the Lost Paradise, Key Concepts in the Practice of Sufism*. A number have also been translated into German, Russian, Albanian, Japanese, Indonesian, and Spanish.

The educational trusts inspired by Gülen have established countless non-profit voluntary organizations—foundations and associations—in Turkey and abroad which support many scholarships.

Though a well-known public figure, Gülen has always shied away from involvement in formal politics. Gülen's admirers include leading journalists, academics, TV personalities, politicians, and Turkish and foreign state authorities. They see in him a true innovator and unique social reformer who practices what he preaches. They see him as a peace activist, an intellectual, a religious scholar, a mentor, author and poet, a great thinker and spiritual guide who has devoted his life to seeking the solutions for society's ills and spiritual needs. They see the movement he helped to nurture as a movement dedicated to education, but an education of the heart and soul as well as of the mind, aimed at reviving and invigorating the whole being to achieve competence and providing goods and services useful to others.

---

* Although official records have listed his date of birth as 1941, the actual date is 1938.

PREFACE

The primary duty of those thinkers that have a clear conscience is to give comprehensive and satisfactory answers to questions that have been raised merely to confuse people's minds; they rack their brains, mining for ideas with the pickax of thought. In a way, this is their raison d'etre. A community without such figures of deep reflection is indeed a poor one. A society whose members have turned their backs on such people can be considered one that has failed to comprehend the purpose of their own existence.

The questions "how" and "why" have existed since the beginning of the world. These are the questions through which the world is given its meaning. This is what we mean when we say "this world is the realm of wisdom." That is, God executes His commands or acts in this world behind the veil of causality. Though God is the Creator and the Ultimate Agent, everything happens according to or within the framework of certain causes. As a matter of fact, inquiring into the relation between cause and effect is wisdom in and of itself. If there were not for the thought-provoking questions (those that are free from evil intentions) how would we be able to talk about wisdom and the All-Wise One?

However, trying to answer every question we face is an unnecessary challenge. When the archangel Gabriel asked the Prophet about when the end of the world would occur, he replied: "The one asked does not know more than the one asking." This answer presents an example of wisdom for us.

To sixty out of every hundred questions asked to him, Imam Abu Yusuf replied "I don't know." Surprised by this, those inquiring retorted, saying: "You are paid to answer our questions, but for the most part you answer 'I don't know.'

How can you explain this?" The great Imam gave them the following meaningful reply: "You are paying me for the things I
know, and if you had paid for what I don't know, the whole
world would not have sufficed."

There is also a proper manner in asking such questions.
Those asked out of genuine wonder and in an acceptable manner are of utmost importance, in our view. Likewise, the
answers to be given to them are very difficult, but critical.

Lazy brains cannot ask good questions. We cannot talk
about action of thought as far as dampened minds are concerned. Another hadith concerning Gabriel teaches us how to
ask. Once, Gabriel appeared in human form and kindly asked
the Prophet for permission to approach him. He asked permission three times, and the fourth time he kneeled, putting his
hands on his knees, and asked again. He then proceeded to ask
critical questions like "What is iman? What is Islam? What is
ihsan?" Gabriel knew the answers to these questions, but his
purpose of disguising himself and posing these questions was to
help others attain this information.

A question is asked for a certain purpose. Asking a question
for the sake of displaying one's own knowledge or asking merely to test the other person is worthless. If a question is asked for
the purpose of learning or in order to let others find out the
information (as in the example of Gabriel above the questioner
may already know the answer), it can be considered a question
that has been posed in the correct manner. Questions of this
kind are like seeds of wisdom. Gabriel's questions are very good
examples. He later went on to affirm the answers that he
received; this signifies his acceptance of the answers as being
correct. In any other case it would not be proper for the person
asking a question to affirm the answer. Moreover, Gabriel was
there to teach the religion and he instantly affirmed that what
the Prophet had said was in full compliance with the Revelation.
Such an affirmation is proper only in such a context.

A good question, i.e. one that is acceptable in terms of manner and intention, inspires the answerer and provides food for thought. Asking is a skill, and answering satisfactorily is a virtue. It is with this in mind that the book you are about to read has been put together.

The first volume addressed to more essential questions concerning Islamic faith; e.g. God and the nature of His existence; can Islam solve every problem? did Prophet Muhammad write the Qur'an? Prophethood; Satan, etc. Although the questions included in this second volume have been selected on the assumption that the reader is already informed of the content of the first volume, an independent reading is still possible for each question-answer is a separate entity and the book does not develop one question upon another.

This book is a translation and like all translations this represents our best attempt to convey the writer's message fairly and clearly. One major problem with the translation of a Turkish text is that it has only one pronoun for the third person and it is not gender-specific as in he or she in English. For reasons of brevity and style, we have settled on the use of "man" in some places, "humanity" or "humankind" in others, where some editors might have preferred "men and women" or a "human being," "a person" or another such expression. The use of the word "man" does not indicate that women are excluded from the author's exhortations, both men and women are addressed.

Muhammed Çetin

CHAPTER 1

Wisdom in the Message
of the Qur'an

1.1.

> It appears that the time of the coming of rain and the sex of the baby in the mother's womb can be known in advance. Are these then no longer to be counted among the "five mysteries" mentioned in the Qur'an?

T he question concerns the mystery of "time" and "knowledge" which governs all five things mentioned in the verse:

> The knowledge of the Hour is with God. It is He Who sends down rain, and He Who knows what is in the wombs. And no one knows what it is that he will earn tomorrow and no one knows in what land he is to die. God is all-knowing, All-Aware. (Luqman 31:34)

Let us look at each of the five briefly in the order given.

God alone knows when and how the Hour, the Resurrection will happen. As the Qur'an states this as a fact and principle, it is improper for a Muslim to offer an opinion on the matter without saying "God knows." We affirm the truth of this from the well-known hadith[1] that tells when the archangel Gabriel came and asked the Prophet to explain *iman*, *Islam*, and *ihsan*. Gabriel confirmed the answers he got by saying *"sadaqta"* (he has spoken truth). Gabriel's last question was: "When will the Resurrection take place?" The Prophet answered, "The one asked does not know more than the one asking." Thereafter, he mentioned certain of the signs and portents of events that would occur close to the time of the Resurrection. Such was the courtesy of the Prophet when asked about one of the "five mysteries." Both the Prophet and Gabriel in fact had some certain knowledge of it, but only God knows when it will happen.

As for how the Resurrection may take place, in terms of likely physical causes, we may surmise many, any of which might suffice to bring it about: such as, a comet striking the earth, or the sun, according to the laws of thermodynamics, extinguishing or exploding, or people may unintentionally initiate some sort of chain reactions beyond their control, and so on and so forth. But, again, only God knows the when and how.

The second "mystery" mentioned in the verse is that it is God who sends down the rain. This is one of the two points raised in the question. People claim to know when it will rain by meteorological analysis, and therefore argue that there is no longer any point in counting rain as one of the mysteries. No doubt some people who put forward such claims have it in mind to generate unease and doubts about the perfection of the Book and the faith. Muslims must nevertheless deal sensitively with such questions, even if they conceal a blasphemous intent.

I begin by asking how much of what people claim to know though modern science and technology is truly related to the unseen or what is beyond our perception. In fact, their guesswork about rainfall, done after all the conditions for it and the signs of it have already begun to be experienced in the visible world, has nothing to do with knowing the Unseen (*ghayb*) at all.

Let me explain this by a simple example. Turn off the ventilation of a room full of people, and introduce some carbon dioxide into the air in the room, measure the oxygen and carbon dioxide levels. Then make a forecast about how many minutes later the people in the room will feel some kind of headache. What if our forecast turns out to be accurate? Will we have known the Unseen? No. The Unseen is defined precisely as that which God assigns only Himself to know. Guessing whether (or roughly where) it will rain tomorrow is not knowing the Unseen. Knowing in all details where, when and how much rain will fall, let's say, in one, five or ten years' time—that would be knowing the Unseen. Let alone in one or five years' time, can people forecast even how much rain will fall the next day? Moreover, we sometimes see that what the meteorologists forecast does not turn out to be accurate; sometimes, even the opposite of what was forecast takes place. That tells us that they do not know for certain, but only make calculated guesses.

Besides, it does not need so many gadgets and apparatuses to know whether the rain, whose symptoms have already become apparent in the visible world (*'alam al-shahada*), will fall or not. There are many common folks who make accurate guesses on the basis of personal experiences acquired over years of observation, and what they say is not less accurate than what the meteorologists say. Let me tell you one of my memories, since it is related to the subject.

Some American scientists came to do research in a village. They saw a shepherd hastily herding his goats back into the fold instead of heading out to the pasture which was in the opposite direction. The scientists were surprised and felt the need to ask why. The shepherd told them it would rain soon and went on with his business. The scientists checked their instruments and saw no chance of a rain. However, it began to rain after a while. The scientists also took refuge in the fold and asked the shepherd how he knew that it would rain. He said, "I have observed over years and learned that the goats lower their tails between their legs before the rain comes." Upon this, some of the scientists despised their expensive gadgets for not being better than a goat's tail! Similarly, Bediüzzaman Said Nursi used to say that due to his rheumatics he felt the rain forty-eight hours in advance. And even some of my fellow-villagers were making correct guesses about whether it would rain or snow by observing the atmospheric symptoms.

Therefore, in the light of hygrometry, hydrostatics, dynamics, meteorology, climatology and other sciences, by observing atmospheric phenomena—the clouds, their density, humidity, change in the air pressure, currents, winds, frontal systems, etc.—and then, using highly sophisticated instruments such as radars, computers and satellites, making forecasts, people are only observing signs and symptoms which are already there and even then only making guesses about the likelihood of rain. Some people seek to present this guesswork as if it were knowing the Unseen, knowing the exact time or amount of the rainfall, and by so doing they pretend to refute the verses of the Qur'an. Their doing so is nothing but a sign of ignorance and impertinence.

I will mention one of the miraculous sayings of the Prophet, which is scientifically accepted today. He said: "No year is more rainy than another."[2] We understand from this hadith that the same amount of rain falls on the world each and every year. However, it is unknown to us where and how much it will rain. That is of the Unseen and cannot be known.

The third thing mentioned in the verse is the second point asked about in the question. It is God Who *knows what is in the wombs*. Some people say that doctors can know what is in the wombs, boy or girl, by ultrasound and other medical procedures. It would be better if they reflected on the fact that to know something whose signs and symptoms have already begun to be experienced in the visible world, has nothing to do with knowing the Unseen at all.

People also claim to be able to predict the sex of an unborn embryo because they can find out the set of sex chromosomes, XX or XY, in the fertilizing sperm. Again, being able to tell the sex chromosomes of a sperm, whether in or out of the womb, has nothing to do with knowing the Unseen. In one of his enlightening sayings, the Prophet said: "If male dominates, it becomes a boy, or if female dominates, it becomes a girl."[3] (This hadith has nothing to do with being dominant in male-female relationships, as wrongly understood by some interpreters in the past.) The fact is that if the sperm with male set of chromosomes (XY) first arrives, manages to penetrate the membrane of the ovum and fertilize it, then it becomes a boy; but if the female set first arrives and does so, then it becomes a girl. Having some certain knowledge about the cause and determining agents of a future event, does not justify any claim to knowing the future in advance; to advance such a claim is sheer self-delusion.

The Qur'an says it is God Who "knows *what* is in the wombs"; it uses the word *ma* here. It does not say it is God Who knows whether it is a boy or a girl in the womb. The "what" relates not merely to the sex of the unborn, but also to the question of whether it will be born at all, and if so, how long it will remain in the womb, whether it will be born alive, what its natural endowments and character will be, its merits or foibles, what sort of a new individual it will be, prosperous believer or wretched evil-doer, what role it will play in life, a blessing or a curse to its parents and society, and the whole entail and outcome of its existence in this world and the Hereafter. To know all these is unique and peculiar to God. So what is truly of the Unseen is here indicated by the inclusive word *ma*, and it is not just a matter of gender. What the Qur'an refers to is comprehensive, general, and universal. Only knowledge of this level could be rightly called knowledge of the Unseen. Claiming the same for anything that humans can and do know is sheer delusion and folly.

To make the point clearer, consider this simple analogy:

Standing on one side of a garden fence, you see an apple tree. The root and trunk of it are on your side, but its branches and leaves are bending over onto the other side, so you are unable to see them. When it is the season to give fruit, you say that the branches on the other side are full of apples now. When people check, they see that it really is so. Does this mean that you knew the Unseen? Or are you just reporting an ordinary event that everyone can normally know? Certainly the latter. This is exactly the same as knowing the sex of the unborn baby in the womb. It is not knowing the Unseen, but merely giving information about a tree whose roots are in the visible world and whose branches are bending into the Unseen. To attempt to invalidate the Qur'anic verse on the basis of such a slight and false claim to knowledge of the Unseen is absolute foolishness.

The fourth point in the verse is "no one knows what he will earn tomorrow." "Earn" here means not only "earn one's livelihood" in a physical and financial sense, but also to reap the consequences (good or ill) of one's conduct generally. Nobody knows what tomorrow may bring forth. All physical and spiritual enlightenment and solace are within this earning. What a scientist adds to his knowledge and experience is also an earning, and God alone knows when and how much it will be. Sometimes you read several volumes of book, but you do not gain a line's worth of knowledge; on the other hand, sometimes a single line may yield to you whole books' worth of knowledge and flood your sources of inspiration.

However, even if we take the reference in only the financial sense, it is not possible to know even how much people on fixed wages will earn tomorrow. For an unexpected gift, or unexpected expenditure, some accident or natural disaster, may dramatically alter the day's earnings. I see no point in giving more examples on this argument and say as the Qur'an says, "no one knows what it is that he will earn tomorrow."

The fifth point is "no one knows in what land he is to die." God alone knows where, when and how one will die. The moment at which Azrail, the archangel of eeath, or his helpers will pronounce "It's time" is unknown to us. As no one raises any objection to this, I leave it there.

The *five mysteries* summed up in the verse are governed by God's Knowledge and Law. We know some things in ordinary life, but this amounts to nothing compared to Divine Knowledge. Our knowledge is made up from superficial acquaintance with certain things, signs and symptoms of which are given from the Unseen to the visible realm. We cannot answer with any precision questions as to when, how or where. This is particularly and acutely clear in the case of rainfall, and human life and death. These remain great mysteries, and full knowledge is with God only.

Verily, God [alone] is All-Knowing, All-Aware.

1.2.

Do the appointed times of death (*ajal*) of people who die *en masse* in natural disasters come to all of them at the same time?

. . . And He knows all that is on land and in the sea; and not a leaf falls but He knows it; and neither is there a grain in the earth's deep darkness, nor anything living or dead, but is recorded in His clear Decree. (An'am 6:59)

Death is understood as the cessation and conclusion of physical existence. The appointed time of death, is the end of the lifetime of each being that lived its own life within the conditions and limits given to it uniquely. Each and every being that came into existence has a beginning, a destined life, and a destined end.

In the flow of time and existence, the difference between a beginning and an end is almost impossible to tell. Every thing that is can be likened to a drop of water which, absorbed by the earth, becomes invisible. Or it may be likened to a stream which flows down to a sea and becomes extinct when it mixes with it. This is the destiny of all beings. They all come into life and pass away according to this destiny.

All beginnings imply their ends; all comings-in are the first point of all goings-out. He that has no beginning has no end, and that One is God, Who is Eternal. It is God Who governs all beings that come into existence within time and He it is Who decrees each individual destiny. He in Himself is free of all increasing and diminishing, of all compounding and decom-pounding, and of birth and death. He is the One Who creates and administers all times, past, present and future. Nothing is that is not under His sovereignty, disposal and power. Therefore, it is not correct to attribute any occurrences to nature alone, without making reference to God, as if to imply that such occurrences are merely natural, that they just happen without Divine Decree. Things are allowed the right to exist only by an Eternal Will and All-Mighty Decree, together with the assign-ment to each of a particular task or service. All creatures, ani-mate or inanimate, come into existence only to serve as mirrors which display the might, power, knowledge and beauty of the One Creator; then, after the appointed time, they are dismissed from the service and give way to newcomers.

All births and deaths work within this framework in order to take their part in this display and to be tested by means there-of. Coming into existence out of nothing indicates the existence of an Unseen Being, and completion of the service and, after a time, dismissal from it, indicate the eternity and the immortali-ty of that Eternal Being Who is not constrained by past or future. Our seeing, hearing and knowing lead the mind to the One Who sees, hears and know all our actions. Our completion of service and thereafter departing this world likewise lead the mind to the Unseen One Who, in contrast, neither enters the creation as we do, nor departs it never to return as we do: *He who created death and life, that He may try which of you is best in deed* (Mulk 67:2).

It is of the utmost importance to understand the secret of coming into and being tested in this world and, therefore, to be ready to depart from it at any time.

Let us now return to the question—do the appointed times of death of people who died *en masse* in natural disasters come to all of them at the same time?

Yes, for those who died so, their appointed time of deaths did come at the same moment. There is no impediment to such an event. The Supreme Being Who possesses and governs the whole creation, Who holds everything under His sovereignty, and Who created everything from the smallest atoms to the largest celestial systems, each with its own destiny, can also destroy each or any number or all of them in an instant. It does not make any difference whether the existent things or beings are in different places, or are of different classes, or have different properties—nor, in respect of His Will, is their number of any significance.

It is possible to say many things to give some notion of the power of the Creator, in order to enable some grasp of what "All-Mighty" means, but it is very difficult to give an exact idea or analogy for it.

Every creature needs energy which in its visible form is light. Every creature depends in some way on the sun to exist and does so in harmony with every other and with the best result. The plant forms achieve their colorful diversity and splendor with the sunlight, and flourish and sink back with sunrise and sunset. Similarly, they all thrive in the spring, bloom in the summer, and fade away in the autumn, enjoying the same destiny harmoniously. Everything comes into existence and its existence is sustained within an all-encompassing, omniscient and omnipotent Will and Plan. Nothing can exist outside of this Divine Decree: . . . *And He knows all that is on land and in the sea; and not a leaf falls but He knows it; and neither is there a grain in the earth's deep darkness, nor anything living or dead, but is recorded in His clear Decree* (An'am 6:59).

If the coming to life, maturing, bearing fruit and dying of the seeds and grains of plant-forms are events so solemnly recorded and stored, can humankind, the most perfect being, be left to live and die, as it were, unattended, unnoticed? The Creator and Owner of all earthly and heavenly realms, Whose hearing and seeing of one thing does not prevent His hearing and seeing of every other thing, will surely attach importance to the deeds and manners of humankind, who is the core of the universe and created in the best stature. The Supreme Being will surely bestow upon humankind, the index of the whole universe, the blessings He bestowed upon the whole creation. He will undoubtedly receive humanity into His Presence and so honor him with a special invitation and unique favor.

This invitation may summon people individually or *en masse*, sometimes in bed, sometimes on a battlefield, and sometimes by means of an accident or disaster. The summons may come at the same moment and in the same way to all people living in one particular place or to different people living in different places and in different ways. Concerning the All-Mighty's dealing with His servants, conditions of time or place or numbers have no relevance. For One Who creates and sends people into this world, Who sustains and cherishes all, Who keeps people in this world as long as He wills and releases them after the completion of their services, it is an easy matter whether He takes souls singly or *en masse*. The latter is no more odd or difficult to understand than that a single word from an army commander can, at a moment pre-arranged by the commander, dismiss a single soldier or the whole army from active service.

Moreover, there is not only one angel commissioned to take the souls of people but many. With the authority, permission and will of their Creator, many angels can meet people and carry out their duties following the Divine Records given to them. In doing so, they approach people, and appear and act to them, in different ways and manners. If particular accidents or disasters are carefully looked at, it will easily be seen that there is indeed a preordination in events, that there is *one* and *only one* appointed time of death, at the same instant, for all those who perished in the particular event. One can find many examples of this reported in the media each day and in books. For example, in earthquakes which turned whole towns upside down, in which adults were unable to save themselves with every sort of means available, babies were dug out of the rubble after many days without any mark or injury; again, when many passengers well able to swim drowned after their vehicles skidded into rivers, babies were found alive, floating on the water; in the same way, there are well-known reports of children found safe and sound thrown meters away from where the plane in which they were traveling crashed and exploded. We could give many such examples; the point is that each and every such incident, every such death or survival, does not just happen. All events take place in accordance with the Eternal Will and All-Mighty Decree of the All-Seeing, All-Hearing and All-Encompassing Creator.

Every being that enters existence, whether alone or *en masse* with others, and then lives until the time for its death appointed in the Record, is commissioned to comprehend the secrets of its primordial nature (*fitra*), to explore the unseen beauties beyond nature, to become a mirror and interpreter to the Creator of the whole. And it may be dismissed from this service, as it entered into it, either singly or *en masse*. Such fore-knowing and register-ing of life, and putting an end to it, is very easy for the Creator. Moreover, God reveals that around each human being there are many angels whose commission is to take souls—in addition to the many other angels with different commissions.

One may ask: Why do some innocent people die in disas-ters along with others who may have deserved such a fate? Such a question arises from false reasoning and an error in belief. If life were only the life in this world, if this world were the first and the last resort of life, that question might be considered a quite sensible and reasonable one. But if this world is a prepar-ing ground and ante-chamber, and the world to come is the fruit and harvest of this one, and a place of rest and felicity, free of toil and hardship, then the question is an aimless one. Given the reality of the life to come, it is not unnatural that good and bad, or righteous and sinner, die together at the same instant in this world. On the contrary, it is quite reasonable and logical for it to be so. For each individual will be resurrected and give an account for what each did, and be chastised or rewarded accord-ing to intentions and deeds.

In sum, death and its time mark the end of life and service in this world. That period of life and its end conform to a pre-ordained plan which, taking human free will into account, is written and stored in the Record. And the Record comes into force whenever its time is due, according to the will and command of the All-Hearing and All-Seeing. There is no difference of principle between whether death comes to a person separately or *en masse* with others.

I suppose that, as in many religious questions, the lack of understanding of the true, limitless knowledge, power and will of the Creator is one of the major reasons for error and doubt. Another reason is a mistaken evaluation of things and events. If, in the face of things and events, one does not eliminate from one's thoughts the mistaken notion of "coincidence" or "nature," if one does not devote oneself to contemplation and religious life and distance oneself from worldly concerns, the inner life will be full of unsound and weak belief and become a battleground for satanic misgivings and anxiety.

While the hearts of people are impoverished and unable to sustain themselves, constant exposure to doubts and misgivings of this nature is profoundly damaging to their spiritual being. In the face of such a situation, one should marvel that the young preserve their faith at all, rather than that they are deviated from it.

It may be claimed that we give too much attention to such issues which may seem, to some people, of little immediate significance in this time. But we cannot agree: any issue related to faith is always of the highest importance and worthy of the most serious effort of reflection and study.

Although Azrail is one, how does he capture the souls of many people who die at the same instant?

By the angels who tear out (the souls of the wicked). By those who gently draw out (the souls of the blessed). And by those who glide along (on errands of mercy). (Nazi'at 79:1-3)

With this question, we again face a subject which, if we tackle it by making human analogies, will mislead us. It is a mistake to liken an angel to a human being, just as it is a mistake to seek the mind in the brain, or the emotions in the heart, or the soul in the body, or—in the language of philosophy—to seek the noumenal in the phenomenal. It would be improper to attempt this question without first pointing out that mistake in thinking and terminology which (probably) is what gives rise to it and other questions like it.

Angels are, as regards their creation and essence, the realm they exist in, and their responsibilities and duties, creatures wholly different from all others. Any argument or judgment made without taking full account of that difference is bound to go wrong. The nature of angels should therefore be approached through consideration of their different creation and essence, their different realm of existence, and their different responsibilities and duties.

Malak (angel) in Arabic relates to *malk* which has the meaning *power*, or to *mal'ak* which has the meaning *messenger*. The shared point of reference is to one most powerful or to the power itself or to one who, as messenger, holds and carries that power: thus, an angel comes to mean one who, as messenger, holds and carries the divine commands. Such an elevated rank belongs to all angels as such. For the angel commissioned to convey the Divine Message to humankind, it is necessary to have the most elevated rank and the most superior attributes of all. Angels are commissioned to oversee all kinds of events—from supervising birth, life, and death to carrying the Throne (*arsh*) and observing the Divine Actions in wonder, admiration and praise. All so-called natural laws, from attraction and repulsion between masses to the principles that regulate electrons spinning around the nucleus, and the putting into effect of these laws, and all changes and transformations, compositions and decompositions, exist under the administration of angels, who are the medium of the messengership and power. Angels are so related to things and events that neither a drop of rain nor a clap of thunder can ever be conceived without them. The laws operating in the universe (*shari'at al-fitriyya*) are the manifestation of the limitless power of the Creator, the All-Mighty, the Absolute Sovereign, on angels according to their skills and capacities. Similarly, all legislative (*tashri'i*) commands to humankind from the attributes of *kalam* are conveyed by angels. Since humanity is the focus of all great and majestic manifestations of the Creator, the Divine inspiration and revelation that come to humanity to guide and regulate his actions are nothing other than the manifestations of God to angels. In this respect, it is ignorance and an error in thinking to liken to human beings, the angelic beings who are a medium or a means between God and His servants, who are charged with supervising or administering all things from atoms to nebulae in dependence on the power of the All-Mighty. It is likewise a misjudgment and an error to consider restrictions by which human existence is bound as applicable also to angels. If the angels had a physical form like that of humankind and were subject to decay and decomposition, if they too were aged and eroded by time, we might use the same criteria for both. However, there is a world of difference which makes such a comparison impossible.

As regards their creation and nature, the angels are different from humankind. The powers and responsibilities of angels are not bounded by space and time. The purity, light (*nur*) and splendor in their essence make them more powerful, influential, quick and active. They can be in touch with many souls, be seen by many eyes, and manifest their oneness in plural forms, at any instant of time or space, even though they are one. In a hadith narrated by 'Aisha, Prophet Muhammad said: "The angels were created out of light (*nur*)."[4] That is why, they are given and thus manifest all the attributes of light.

Luminous things, like the sun, though single, are reflected by and so seen in each transparent object; they can reach and be seen by each and every eye. Similarly, the angels, who are created out of light, can meet and be reflected in many souls; and they can deal with thousands of them at an instant. The angels, whose essence is *latif* (fine, subtle), are very different from what has material form and is therefore heavy and dense. The angels can take different shapes and forms; also, they can be seen in different shapes and forms at the same instant. *Tamassul*, the souls' or angels' assuming visible forms, has long been known among religious people, and there are many examples of it. It is even now not uncommon to hear claims (something, alas, of a pastime among the so-called "idle rich") of some individual's "spirit" or "double" being in a place separate and distant from where the body is and able to produce material effects. Whatever the truth of such reports and claims, they indicate that all fine beings like souls, in comparison to physical beings, are more capable, quick and active. Angels are far more capable, quick and active than souls, which is another indication that angels operate beyond the bounds of physical nature.

As we said, *tamassul* of souls and angels is a phenomenon that has long been known and reported. The Prophets in the first place and then the saints have recounted their experiences, and many ordinary people around them witnessed such incidents. The coming and appearance of the archangel Gabriel, in different guises and personalities, according to the reasons and missions he was given, such as being a messenger while conveying the Revelations and being a warrior during battles, are good examples of *tamassul*: Gabriel appeared in the form of Dihya[5]; as another angel, whose name we do not know, fought till evening in front of the Prophet as Mus'ab ibn 'Umayr[6]; many angels took part in the battle of Badr in the guise of Zubayr ibn Awwam to boost the morale of the Muslims.[7]

There are many incidents which indicate that some saints are in touch with the heroes of the Unseen, among them former saints and Companions of the Prophet. Also, their appearance to ordinary people in dreams and trance-like states supports the argument. A number of godly men and women have testified that, in their dreams, particular noble souls always keep in touch with them, and give them guidance. To be sure, there will be people who refer all such experiences to the "subconscious" and so make the whole subject incomprehensible. Alas for their ignorance and arrogance!

To sum up what we have said so far: just as all beings are seen reflected in a mirror, so angels are seen in everything that can be a mirror to them, but with this difference that angels are not merely a picture or image, as a reflection in a mirror is, but are as themselves, with all their powers and faculties. Like a beam of light, angels can reach and be in various places at the same time and carry out their duties, the distance of the place or the number of people concerned are of no relevance and can present no hindrance. The sun is single but is reflected, seen, and its effects are felt, everywhere on every object according to the object's qualities. Similarly, the angels, being created of light, can be seen, breathe life into human beings or recapture their souls or carry out any other of their duties everywhere at any time.

In reality it is, of course, God who gives and takes life. Azrail is only a medium and means, commissioned to superintend the giving of life and recapturing of souls and to praise the All-Mighty in His Divine Actions. As God is everywhere at every instant and performs innumerable actions beyond the power of our imaginations to conceive, it is not difficult to accept that He can create, give and take innumerable lives all in a single instant. Such omniscience and omnipotence can undoubtedly see, administer and govern the deeds, and give and take the lives, of as many people as there may be particles in the whole universe, at the same instant, though some unfortunate atheists may refuse to believe.

Whether God or Azrail captures the souls, each soul whose time of death has come turns to God at its last moment and then is taken. We can make this more comprehensible by an analogy. Let us suppose that there are thousands of radio-like receivers operating on the same frequency. If any transmitter sends signals on that frequency, they will be heard on all the receivers. In the same way, all beings live in dependence for everything on the All-Mighty, All-Generous Creator, and when they ask for anything from Him, they do so through their poverty, that is, through their needs, their helpless impotence. And when they reach the last minute of their life and turn to God by, as it were, switching on to their life-ending frequency, they begin to perceive the signals of death. If a weak, powerless human being can make contact with systems hundreds of miles away simply by pressing a button, why cannot the All-Mighty Creator, who is free from all our weakness, impotence and deficiencies, make contact with souls, each of which is, in a sense, a living machine? Why cannot He make them all start or stop functioning in an instant?

Summary

1. It is God who gives and takes life. Azrail is only an agent who is commissioned to oversee and administer and praise the work of God.

2. While carrying out his task, Azrail acts only with the permission and approval of God.

3. As a great number of angels administer tasks in the universe as representatives of the Divine Authority, Power and Will, there are many angels that can help Azrail with his work. They

are even grouped into classes according to their tasks. Some of them take the lives of people without causing them any distress or hurt—they carry out their task peacefully. After souls have been recaptured, other angels at once take the souls before the Divine Presence, and so on. The Qur'an refers to all of them: *By the angels who tear out (the souls of the wicked). By those who gently draw out (the souls of the blessed). And by those who glide along (on errands of mercy)* (Nazi'at 79:1-3).

Thus there are different angels dispatched according to the level of the people they will deal with. They are all under the supervision of Azrail, and God commissions them according to whether the individuals concerned were good or wicked.

In conclusion, we can say that the understanding which gives rise to such questions begins in an error of thinking in that it mistakenly likens angels to human beings. We have pointed out that angels are quite different from beings with physical form; not only in their essence and creation but also in their tasks, servanthood and responsibilities, angels are quite different from other creatures. Angels can assume different forms (*tamassul*), be in many places, and do many things, as human beings' souls can. What is popularly read about in our day in connection with spirit-mediums, necromancy, and other such efforts to communicate with the Unseen, are in their way evidence of metaphysical elements operating in the physical universe. Angels, as beings far superior to these elements, can function and carry out their missions in a way far superior to all other beings. And certainly, at the time of death, when people share the same "frequency" with the angels, an angel can deal with thousands of people at the same instant. Finally, we must remember that the angel for death is not alone; rather, there are innumerable angels appointed for taking souls, and when we consider that there is an angel for each individual death, no further point remains to raise the kind of doubts expressed in the question.

God knows best.

I.4.

What is the wisdom in fasting?

The hawk's swooping contributes to the sparrow's alertness and agility. Although rain, electricity, or fire sometimes harms people, no one curses them. Fasting may be difficult, but it provides the body with energy, activity, and resistance. A child's immune system usually gains strength through illness. Gymnastics are not easy, but they are almost essential to bodily health and strength. People's spirits are refined through worship and meditation as well as through illness, suffering, and hardship. These allow them to acquire Paradise, for God gives a large reward for a little sacrifice. Hardships and sufferings promote people to higher spiritual degrees, and will be returned manifold in the other world. This is why all Messengers experienced the most grievous hardships and sufferings.

Hardship, suffering, and calamity cause believers' sins to be forgiven, warn them away from sins and the seductions of Satan and the carnal self, help them appreciate God's blessings, and open the way to gratitude. Also, they urge the rich and healthy to be concerned about the ill and the poor and to help them. Those who have never suffered cannot understand the condition of those who are hungry, sick, or stricken with a calamity. In addition, these afflictions may help establish closer relations between different social sectors.

The role of intention in fasting

Intention has a prominent place in our actions, for God's Messenger told us that our actions are judged according to our intentions. Intention is the spirit of our actions, for without it there is no reward. If you remain hungry and thirsty from daybreak to sunset without intending to fast, God does not consider it a fast. If you fast without intending to obtain God's good pleasure, you receive no reward. So whatever one intends, one gets the reward thereof. Those who have a firm belief in God, the other pillars of faith, and the intention to believe in them will be rewarded with eternal felicity in Paradise. But those who are determined not to believe, who have removed the inborn tendency to believe from their hearts, will be victims of their eternal determination and deserve eternal punishment. As for those with deeply ingrained unbelief and who have lost the capacity to believe, we read in the Qur'an: *As for the unbelievers, it is the same whether you warn them or warn them not. They will not believe. God has set a seal on their hearts and on their hearing, and on their eyes there is a covering* (Baqara 2:6-7).

Favoring the Heart as Opposed to the Flesh

Human life is a composite of two distinct powers: the spirit and the flesh. Although they sometimes act in harmony, conflict is more usual—conflict in which one defeats the other. If bodily lusts are indulged, the spirit grows more powerless as it becomes more obedient to those lusts. If one can control the desires of the flesh, place the heart (the seat of spiritual intellect) over reason, and oppose bodily lusts, he or she acquires eternity.

Compared with previous centuries, people may well be wealthier and enjoy more convenience and comfort. However, they are trapped in greed, infatuation, addiction, need, and fantasy much more than ever before. The more they gratify their animal appetites, the more crazed they become to gratify those appetites; the more they drink, the thirstier they get; the more they eat, the hungrier they get. They enter into evil speculations to feed their greed to earn still more, and sell their spirits to Satan for the most banal advantages. And so they break with true human values a little more each day.

To sacrifice one's enjoyment of worldly pleasures has the same significance for human progress as roots have for a tree's growth. Just as a tree grows sound and strong in direct relation to its roots' soundness and strength, people grow to perfection whose striving to free themselves from selfishness so that they can live for others.

Spiritual practices during Ramadan

Muhasaba (Self-Criticism or Self-Interrogation)

Self-criticism may be described as seeking and discovering one's inner and spiritual depth, and exerting the necessary spiritual and intellectual effort to acquire true human values and to develop the sentiments that encourage and nourish them. This is how one distinguishes between good and bad, beneficial and harmful, and how one maintains an upright heart. Furthermore, it enables a believer to evaluate the present and prepare for the future. Again, self-criticism enables a believer to make amends for past mistakes and be absolved in the sight of God, for it provides a constant realization of self-renewal in one's inner world. Such a condition enables one to achieve a steady relationship with God, for this relationship depends on a believer's ability to live a spiritual life and remain aware of what takes place in his or her inner world. Success results in the preservation of one's celestial nature as a true human being, as well as the continual regeneration of one's inner senses and feelings.

Tafakkur (Reflection)

Reflection is a vital step in becoming aware of what is going on around us and of drawing conclusions from it. It is a golden key to open the door of experience, a seedbed where the trees of truth are planted, and the opening of the pupil of the heart's eye. Due to this, the greatest representative of humanity, the foremost in reflection and all other virtues states: "No act of worship is as meritorious as reflection. So reflect on God's bounties and the works of His Power, but do not try to reflect on His Essence, for you will never be able to do that."[8] By these words, in addition to pointing out the merit of reflection, the glory of humankind determines the limits of reflection and reminds us of our limits.

Shukr (Thankfulness)

True thankfulness in one's heart is manifested through the conviction and acknowledgment that all bounties are from God, and then ordering one's life accordingly. One can thank God verbally and through one's daily life only if personally convinced, and if one willingly acknowledges that his or her existence, life, body, physical appearance, and all abilities and accomplishments are from God, as are all of the bounties obtained and consumed. This is stated in: *Do you not see that God has made serviceable unto you whatsoever is in the skies and whatsoever is in the earth, and has loaded you with His bounties seen or unseen?* (Luqman 31:20), and: *He gives you of all that you ask Him; and if you reckon the bounties of God, you can never count them* (Ibrahim 14:34).

Of course, one should try to increase in all virtues during Ramadan, as this is the best time of year to do so.

Why does the Qur'an mention a person such as Abu Lahab who was an inveterate enemy of Islam? What is the wisdom in doing so? How does it befit the dignity and purport of the Divine Book?

Abu Lahab was one of the uncles of Prophet Muhammad, peace and blessings be upon him. His real name was 'Abd al-Uzza. He was popularly called Abu Lahab (literally, "the father of flame") on account of his ruddy complexion and hot, fiery temper. He was one of the most inveterate enemies of early Islam. His hostility came from his inborn arrogance, pride in his great wealth and children, and a dislike of the messages the Prophet conveyed. Abu Lahab's wife, Umm Jamil, was equally vehement in her spite and cruelty against the Prophet and his followers. Her hatred was so intense that, in order to cause the Prophet bodily injury, she would often make up bundles of thorns with ropes of twisted palm fiber and, under the cover of darkness, strew them around his house and on the paths he was expected to take. Also, she used her considerable wealth and great eloquence in persistently slandering the Prophet and his message.

At that early time of Islam, the Prophet called the people to come together and listen to his preaching and warning. When they had assembled, he asked them, "If I were to inform you that enemy warriors are about to fall upon you from behind that hill, would you believe me?" They answered, "Yes, we would."

Thereupon he said, "Behold, then, I am here to warn you of the coming of the Last Hour." At that, Abu Lahab flared up and cursed the Prophet, saying, "Did you summon us here just for this? May you perish!" Shortly after that incident the chapter *Masad* (111th chapter, also called *Tabbat*) was revealed, which derives its name from its last word, *masad* (the twisted strands). It is the sixth in the order of revelation and relates to the bitter hostility always shown to the Prophet's message by Abu Lahab.

> Perish the hands of the father of flame! Perish he! No profit to him from all his wealth, and all his gains! Burnt soon will he be in a fire of blazing flame. His wife shall carry the (kindling) wood as fuel; A twisted rope of palm-leaf fiber round her neck. (Masad 111)

Abu Lahab and his wife used their will and wealth in the wrong way. Though they lived very close to the Prophet, they never tried to understand his message. While the Prophet and the Muslims were marching toward the Ka'ba, they scattered thorns and set up fires to prevent their progress. They spent their life in unrelenting rage and hatred, cruel plots and persecutions; their punishment was to be the same kind as what they had relentlessly inflicted on Muslims.

Abu Lahab was unable to take part in the Battle of Badr. He was sitting in a large tent near the Ka'ba when the news of the battle was brought to him. When he was told how "men in white with turbans on piebald horses between heaven and earth" had helped the Muslims and fought against the unbelievers, he was greatly shaken. Umm al-Fadl, 'Abbas' wife, and Abu Rafi', 'Abbas' slave, were among those who listened to the same news in the corner of the tent. They were both Muslims who had kept their Islam secret from all but a few. But Abu Rafi' could not contain himself for joy at the news of the Prophet's victory. On hearing of "the turbaned men in white, between heaven and earth," he exclaimed, "By God, those were the angels!" An impulse of maddening rage seized Abu Lahab who struck Abu

Rafi' in the face, bore him to the ground, knelt over him and struck him repeatedly. Then Umm al-Fadl took up a wooden pole used to reinforce the tent posts, and brought it down with all her strength on Abu Lahab's head, heavily wounding him. "Will you treat him as of no account, now that his master is away and cannot protect him?" she cried. Since she was his sister-in-law, Abu Lahab did not say anything to her and went home directly. His wound did not heal, but putrefied. As a result of this blow or for other reasons, he was infected with a disease called *adasa* (malignant measles, black measles), at that time considered to be more deadly than plague. His wealth, his position, or his children were of no avail. Even his own wife and the children, of whom he had always boasted, abandoned him. His whole body was covered with festering pustules. After writhing in pain for a week, he died with no one to attend his deathbed. No one came to remove his dead body from the house until, eventually, his embarrassed relatives hired some Bedouins from the desert, and had them take the rotten corpse out, throw it to a pit and heap some stones on it.

Not only did Abu Lahab not benefit from the Prophet, in spite of his kinship with him, he became his most inveterate enemy. Therefore, a terrible end and punishment in both this world and the next were his due. His hands, the instruments of his action, perished, and he perished himself. His words, power and influence proved futile.

Umm Jamil came from the noble and wealthy family of Banu Umayyad. She never held back from any of the cruel and unrelenting persecutions inflicted upon the Prophet and the Muslims; rather, she took a deep, even malicious, pleasure in them. She collected and carried thorns, scrub and pieces of wood to scatter and make fire on the ways the Prophet was likely to take. "Carrying fire wood" may also be a metaphor for "carrying tales" between people to embroil them, another of her vices. Though excessively fond of ostentatious luxury and of using servants, her rage against the Prophet and Islam was such that she disregarded her pride in her high rank and stooped to work that, in those days, was done by only slaves and servants. Instead of necklaces and jewelry, she took delight in putting the rope of twisted palm fiber around her neck with which she carried thorns and wood on her back to use against the Prophet. Her punishment in the Hereafter would be of the same kind as what she relentlessly inflicted on Muslims in this world. The Qur'an implies as such.

Abu Lahab was a particularly determined, stubborn person. Abu Jahl, who knew this side of Abu Lahab's character, would say, "Never enrage him. If he should join the other side [i.e. the Muslims], no one will ever be able to turn him back." Unfortunately, Abu Lahab used this strength of determination in enmity against the Prophet. He and his wife both revered the idols at the Ka'ba. They never gave a thought to the Prophet's teaching, even though he was a near relative, one raised in their immediate neighborhood and known to everyone (including themselves) for steadiness of character, impeccable honesty, and trustworthiness. While they had not the least idea that their kinsman and neighbor was chosen by God as His Last Messenger to humankind, they certainly knew no wrong of him, nor had they suffered any harm at his hands. Nevertheless, they determined, in the most resolute and spiteful way, to do him injury and harm to the extent of their influence and power.

Abu Jahl, a close ally and associate of Abu Lahab, organized the three-year economic and social boycott against the Muslims in Makka. The boycott forbade any trade or any contract of marriage between the Muslims and idolaters. Some of the elderly and the very young among the Muslims died as a result of the hardships, physical and mental, imposed upon them. Alas, their sufferings did not stir the least bit of sadness or compassion in Abu Lahab.

The Prophet's wife, Khadija (*umm al-mu'minun*—mother of believers), died at that time. In the same year, later known as the "year of sadness," died another uncle of the Prophet, Abu Talib, beloved by him, and who was the Muslims' most significant and reliable protector. But for the authority and influence of Abu Talib, the idolaters in Makka would not have hesitated to kill the Messenger outright. However, though he protected the Muslims as kinsfolk, as best he could, Abu Talib himself did not embrace Islam. He was one of those whom the Prophet particularly desired should believe. When Abu Talib was on his deathbed, the Messenger again invited him to belief, but idolaters like Abu Jahl and Abu Lahab surrounded him so as to prevent his embracing Islam. The Prophet was deeply grieved that Abu Talib had passed away in unbelief.

On the day of the conquest of Makka, Abu Bakr, the closest Companion of the Prophet, took his aged father who had then accepted Islam to God's Messenger. As he did so, Abu Bakr sobbed bitterly. Later, he explained:

> O Messenger of God, I desired very much that my father should believe, and now he has believed. But I desired the belief of Abu Talib even more than that because you desired it. That is why I am weeping.

Whereas Abu Talib did everything he could to protect the Prophet, Abu Talib's brother, Abu Lahab encouraged and took part in all sorts of cruelties against the Prophet and the Muslims.

When the Prophet went from clan to clan inviting the people to the principle that all human beings are equal before God and will be judged by Him on their merits alone, one man, with red beard and complexion would follow him like a shadow and seek to undermine the impression he made on audiences. Whereas people from the farthest clans and tribes came to affirm some form of kinship or other with the Prophet, Abu Lahab considered getting far away from him as almost a duty, an obligation. It is of one so willfully blind that he refused even the light of the sun rising around him, that the Qur'an declared, *Perish the hands of Abu Lahab!*

There are several verses in the Qur'an that allude directly or indirectly to people who did whatever they could to abuse and persecute the Prophet, to run down his doctrine, and to injure those who believed in him. One of these inveterate enemies was Walid ibn Mughira, father of Khalid soon to become Islam's first great military commander. Walid was pondering ways to slander the Prophet and to undermine the wonderful influence that the Qur'anic verses had on their listeners. He hesitated over which accusation to use, whether "poet" or "magician" or "soothsayer." Eventually he determined in favor of saying "magic" of the Qur'an and "magician" of the Prophet. To this incident, the Qur'an refers in the verse:

> . . . And Woe to him! How he determined! . . . (Muddathir 74:19)

Other unbelievers are reproached and threatened in other verses. That being so, there is no reason why Abu Lahab should have been excepted. Indeed, if Abu Lahab had not been reproached whereas Walid ibn Mughira had been, some people are bound to have wondered if Abu Lahab was spared just because of his familial relationship to the Prophet. But the Qur'an did not give any grounds for such a notion; it included Abu Lahab in the same category as all the idolatrous unbelievers.

The chapter naming Abu Lahab was revealed in Makka, well before the battle of Badr. The Qur'an said that Abu Lahab and his wife would die as unbelievers, and so it happened just a week after Badr. Before the fighting at Badr, the Prophet walked around the battlefield and pointed to particular locations, saying, "Abu Jahl will be killed here, Utba here, Shayba here, Walid here,"[9] and so on. After the battle the Companions found the corpses where it had been predicted they would be. This served to boost the morale of the believers at a time when they were few and their enemies too many. In a similar way the prediction and the fact of Abu Lahab's death served to increase the believers' morale and became a caution, a stern forewarning, to all.

Sometimes an understanding or self-knowledge gained through a slight misfortune or calamity can lead to a spiritual attainment such that (if the veil of the Unseen is lifted and one sees what he has gained) one would ask for the misfortune and calamity to recur, because in comparison to what is gained ultimately, the misfortune or calamity amount to very little. On the other hand, there are people whose humanity is so destroyed, who have doomed themselves to losing it perpetually, that they cannot gain anything from misfortunes. Whether the Qur'an does or does not use dire, threatening language about them will not affect in the slightest degree the course or consequences of their actions, or their ends. Those people determined and prepared their own irreversible end. The Qur'an's specific mentioning of Abu Lahab and his wife strike some readers as inappropriate to the dignity of a Divine scripture. But, over the centuries the verses have encouraged millions of people to reflect upon their intentions and actions, to seek to avoid falling into the condition of Abu Lahab and his wife, to encourage each other on the path of right actions. Thus, there is much wisdom in the naming such in these verses; psychologically and pedagogically it has proved to be useful and necessary for the benefit of the believers.

At the same time the chapter produced doubts and misgivings on the part of the unbelievers. By turning their fixed, secure unbelief into doubts and misgivings, it made coming to Islam easier for them. The affirmation of faith, too long imprisoned in their consciousness, was able to penetrate into their hearts and minds. Many people forsook their once resolute unbelief and became Muslim, and started to guide, instruct and enlighten others.

In short, specifically mentioning a couple who were notorious for their determined enduring hatred of Islam, expounding the Divine wrath that persistent hatred incurs and specifically indicating the outcome for that couple, is not an example of a failure of substance or style. On the contrary, it is evidence of and another example of the profundity and marvelous variety of the Qur'an's methods and meanings. It is like throwing a small stone into an ocean and producing an endless sequence of waves all over that ocean. That sequence of waves has been continually causing the hearts of millions of people to be moved. The

Qur'an was revealed in such a lofty style that by informing of an individual's death in unbelief in a way that balances attraction and repulsion, the chapter became a means for millions of people to attain guidance. Its meaning is much wider than its reference in the first instance to two specific individuals. This befits and conforms to the eloquence, clarity and the purport of the Qur'an, which is the very wisdom and appropriateness.

CHAPTER 2

Ethics and Spirituality

2.1.

What is *ulfa* (familiarity)? And what are its negative effects?

The word *ulfa* means familiar intercourse, familiarity, friendship. But what is meant in the question has a far broader and more comprehensive meaning than the bare translation of the word conveys.

Humanity's relationship to things and events, the meanings and conclusions drawn by them from such relationship, the actions and reactions that are aroused by these conclusions within their conscience, and the changes in their actions and attitudes as a result of all these, are a chain of matters that keep their souls alert, active, sensitive and vigorous.

The admiration humanity feel for the splendor and attraction of the creation, the curiosity and wonder they feel about the precise operation and order of the universe, the gains they make from the things they discover, the urge to acquire more and more, and the intellectual capacity and the organized way of their thinking, lead them to be mentally and spiritually sensitive, alert, active for and preoccupied with all events.

By contrast, if they do not perceive the exciting beauties and varieties of things and events around them, but go on living unaware of the harmonious combinations working in the universe, inattentive and indifferent to everything around them; if they do not seek for the cause and effect and wisdom behind all things and events; and also, if they do not discover their inner

world and soul—this shows insensitivity, negligence and ignorance, and spiritual enervation. Neither the mysterious book of
the universe nor the opening out before their gaze of its signs,
leaf by leaf, teaches him anything. *And how many signs in the
heavens and the earth do they pass by? Yet they turn (their faces)
away from them!* (Yusuf 12:105). In spite of exposure to falls and
rises, to such convincing illustrations in nature and history, how
few people really benefit from them!

For those who are aware of what is going on around them,
their curiosity and wonder at the creation are like setting forth
on an endless sea, in each stage of which they acquire the gold-
en keys to the mysterious palaces of the universe. As they
advance with pure heart, elevated feelings, composed mind and
soul ready to receive inspirations, and as they feed their soul
with what they gather from the whole creation, their intellectual world turns to a garden of Paradise and yields its fruits.

Those who do not acquire such an understanding cannot
take themselves out of the circle of familiarity and keep com-
plaining about the monotony of things and events. According
to such people, everything is chaos, dark and meaningless. . . .
Even if they see all the signs, they will not believe in them. . . (A'raf
7:146). Their minds are chained, their souls yoked, and *their
hearts are sealed, so they understand not* (there are many verses in
the Qur'an ending this way). Such people cannot be expected to
do any good or produce anything useful. It is impossible to
hope for something from them in this mood.

There is another sort of familiarity which happens after one
has fully known and realized something or supposed that one
has, though, in reality, one has not. This is what the question was
getting at. After having known, believed, acquired or experienced a little, the changing conditions and the renewed beauties
should result in new dimensions and greater profundity. To lose
one's interest, alertness and sensitivity and to no longer draw lessons or conclusions, is a kind of fall or deviation, of decay and
death, in one's feelings.

If those who have fallen into such a situation do not waken immediately and run (or are not led to run) to appreciate again the delicacy, subtlety of thought and wisdom in things; if they do not open their ears, listen to, and understand, the Divine Messages, they are destined to become barren and perish. Therefore, the Creator of the universe has sent many and various people and given lessons and warnings by them. By these sincere, reliable, eloquent, and infallible guides, the Almighty reiterates His Eternal Messages and thus brings clarity to the minds, strength to the hearts, and peace to the souls. Moreover, He always awakens consciences against that to which they may get habituated, and urges people to review all the tableaux He presents to their understanding.

God reiterates many times the creation of humanity, the dispersal of humankind over the farthest corners of the world, their union and happiness with their mates, the grandeur and magnificence in the creation of the world and heavens, the variations in languages and colors, the alternations of day and night, and the blessings, fertility and prosperity that come with climatic activities such as thunderstorms, lightning and rain, in most powerful and varied words. God never leaves any room for "becoming habituated" for over-familiarity—at least, not for those of His servants who know, reflect, reason, and understand.

> Among His signs is this, that He created you from dust and then— Behold, you are men scattered (far and wide)! And among His signs is this that He created for you mates from among yourselves, that you may dwell in tranquility with them, and He has placed love and mercy between your (hearts): In that are signs for those who reflect. And among his signs is the creation of the heavens and the earth, and the variations in your languages and your colors. In that are signs for those who know. And among His signs is the sleep that you take by night and by day, and the quest that you (make for livelihood) out of His bounty. In that are signs for those who hearken. And among His signs, He shows you the lightning, by way both of fear and of hope, and He sends down rain from the sky and with it gives

life to the earth after it is dead. In that are signs for those who
are wise. (Rum 30:20-4)

Like the above, many Qur'anic verses draw our attention to
the extraordinary wonders and miracles that a great number of
human beings pass by each day without taking lessons from
them. Our situation may be likened to that of a fish that lives in
the water but does not know what water is nor how valuable it
is for itself.

Another form of *ulfa*, over-familiarity is that staleness in
one's thinking and mentality that affects one's actions and worship. This is the death of one's love (*'ishq*), ecstasy (*wajd*), and
enthusiasm. One who falls into such a state loses the love and
excitement for worship, the sense of responsibility, the aversion
to sins, and the liking for repentance and lamenting sins. From
then on, it is almost impossible to turn that person into his former good state. It requires very pure and sincere persons to
remind and help that person to look to himself, so that he can
evaluate his situation and heed the warnings and the people who
give those warnings.

Each and every voice and breath that comes to humankind
to establish a new spirit has always conveyed the same message:
To become habituated, dull, stale, to grow old and become
corpse-like is inevitable for some people at some time, but it is
never impossible to reform, as long as they are respectful to
those who must use a sharp instrument to cure their sickness:

> Has not the time arrived for the believers that their hearts in all
> humility should engage in the remembrance of God and of the
> Truth which has been revealed, and that they should not become
> like those to whom was given the Book aforetime, but long ages
> passed over them and their hearts grew hard? For many among
> them are rebellious and transgressors. (Hadid 57:16)

In sum, *ulfa*, staleness and over-familiarity, is a great disaster which afflicts human beings, and has in fact afflicted many.
The afflicted person is unaware of the happenings around him,

blind to the beauties in the great book of the universe, and deaf to the tongues which speak of the truth. That is why he is shallow and inadequate in his faith, without any love and ecstasy in his worship, and unbalanced, unjust and erring in his social relations. His rescue from such a situation depends on a powerful hand stretched out to help him and make him see and hear again. For this reason, such a person should be made to reflect and meditate on death and the Hereafter, to visit many charity and service institutions, to take part in some social and religious service, to study and review the glorious pages of the history of Islam and thus look up to the heroes of Islam, to meet with sincere, well-versed, people full of Islamic love, ecstasy, and zeal. In this way, the opportunities and conditions should be prepared to reform and renew that person. There are many more points to make on this subject, but we have had time only to review some of them in the hope, and with the prayer, that God, the All-Mighty, in Whose hands are the keys to all hearts, may remove *ulfa* from ours.

What is "unity of being" (*wahdat al-wujud*)? Does it conform in any way to the teachings of Islam?"

Wahdat al-wujud (literally, oneness or unity of being) is a teaching mostly spoken of in connection with mystics and Sufis. Although the phrase refers to a subjective state or direct, inward experience attained by Sufis, it has also been understood and discussed as a philosophical concept and, as such, interpreted in different ways. Some have even considered it practically indistinguishable from *wahdat al-mawjud* (the oneness or unity of existents), a philosophy known in the West by the name monism.

As with much else, *wahdat al-wujud* has reached us with excesses and extremes in the use and understanding of it. In some cases because of lack of suitable words to express the experience to which it alludes; in others because of inadequacies in the manner in which the phrase has been applied to the ordinary, visible reality of this world; in yet others because it inclines to a line of thought very like another philosophical doctrine, namely pantheism—the phrase *wahdat al-wujud* which, strictly speaking, can only be referred to God Himself, has been conceived and interpreted in diverse ways and led to a variety of unsound speculations and controversies.

Those who uphold the teaching of *wahdat al-wujud* distinguish three modes of *tawhid* (oneness):

1. *Tawhid al-af'al (oneness or unity of the Agent):* Meaning that, of every act, the sole and only, the absolute, Agent is God.

It follows from this view that there is no need to look for any cause for whatever exists or happens in the universe; everything everywhere is directly the work of God. (Since we dealt with the issue of *kasb* (the performance or doing of acts) and *khalq* (the createdness of acts), matters pertaining to *kalam* (theology), in the questions related to destiny, we shall not repeat that discussion here.) Those who argue for *tawhid al-af'al* cite the following verses to support their view:

> But God has created you and what you do. (Saffat 37:96) . . .
> All is from God . . . (Nisa 4:78)

2. Tawhid al-sifat (oneness or unity of the Subject): Meaning that of all predicates the sole and only Subject is God. According to this view, all volition, all forces and powers, all knowledge and faculties, belong to God only; they are an intelligible expression, or a work, or a realized state of Him.

3. Tawhid al-dhat (also, tawhid al-wujud) (oneness or unity of Essence or of Being): Meaning that in essence all existence is One; and everything visible or knowable around us, other than Him, is a manifestation and disclosure of Him in certain states.

There is much to say and dispute about here, from the modes of *tawhid* to the subtle nuances between manifestation and disclosure. However, since the question asked here concerns only the third mode of *tawhid,* we will only dwell upon the *tawhid al-dhat* (oneness or unity of Essence or Being).

Given that such a view of *tawhid,* as noted above, is the result of an inward state or direct, inward experience (*dhawq*), many scholars do not consider the subject amenable to rational discussion.

In fact, when existents and events are not referred ultimately to God and His Names, it is impossible to explain them fully. That is acknowledged by all people of sound learning who reflect seriously and pursue their reflections fully. There is considerable similarity between the understanding of *tawhid* of those who use rational methods of inquiry, and those who follow the disciplines of Sufism. Sa'd al-Din Taftazani, in his *Sharh al-Maqasid* (Explanation of Purposes), distinguishes two groups among those who argue *wahdat al-wujud*, of whom one he assesses to be within the bounds of the *ahl al-Sunna*, i.e. orthodox: there is no dispute about or with this group.

According to Taftazani, the two groups are the *sufiyya* and *mutasawwifa*. The former hold to the plurality in *wujud* as is in *mawjud*, in essential being as in existence. However, when the Sufi reaches God, he is immersed in the ocean of *'irfan* (perception, direct knowing); he experiences *fana'*, the perishing or loss of the self in God and of his attributes in God's attributes. As a result of this mystical experience, he believes that nothing exists other than God; he regards himself as the focus (*mikhraq*) of all manifestation (*tajalli*) of the Divine Attributes: this is the state the Sufis call *fana' fi l-tawhid* or perishing into the Oneness. Unable at this point to understand the reality of the situation, the Sufis may exclaim in ecstatic utterances a condition of indwelling (*hulul*) in God or of "union" (*ittihad*) with God.

According to some Sufis, such an understanding of *tawhid* is the result of that stage or degree of union with God (*maqam al-jam*). But this is firstly a matter of *'irfan*, and then a matter of experience or tasting (*dhawq*). In this degree, attributing real existence to things could not but be contradictory to the Sufis' visions (*mushahadat*). That is why, to acknowledge *asbab* (causes) in that state would be, in a sense, to acknowledge an associate with God (i.e. to do *shirk*). On the other hand, to deny the *asbab* without really attaining such a degree of consciousness, without really experiencing it fully, is hypocrisy and a merely theoretical assertion. Therefore, one who denies union (*jam'*) is considered *'irfan*-less (unknowing, unperceiving) and one who denies the difference between God and humankind (*farq*) which the Sufi overcomes in the experience of *jam'* is considered far away from the secrets of servanthood to God. The mature person is one who comfortably accepts both *farq* and *jam'*, each in its necessary place.

The second group comprise those who argue an absolute *wahdat al-wujud*. For them Being is One, which is nothing other than God. The multiplicity of the visible is only imaginary or illusory.

While *wahdat al-wujud* is for the *sufiyya* a matter of affective state (*hal*) or direct experience (*dhawq*), the *mutasawwifa* seem to hold to it as an established conviction and philosophy. In fact, not a few theologians have shared that conviction. Some of them, such as Jalal al-Din Dawwani, have defended it vigorously. However, the general consensus of *ahl al-Sunna* scholars is that the (separate) reality of things in the world is *thabit* (securely established).

Sheikhulislam M. Sabri in his *Mawqif al-'aql* (The Station of Reason) indicates that the concept of *wujud al-haqq* (unity or oneness of reality) is behind that of *wahdat al-wujud*. But, as is known and accepted by scholars and theologians, *wujud* is an addition to *mahiyya* (quiddity); this is so both in that which is *wujub* (necessary) and that which is *mumkin* (possible). However, Imam al-Ash'ari held the opposite, namely that *wujud* is the same as *mahiyya* both in *wujub* and *mumkin*. While the Philosophers agree with al-Ash'ari in regard to *wujub*, they side with theologians in regard to *mumkin*. Since the schools of al-Ash'ari and the Philosophers consider *wujud* to be ultimately from God Himself and from His Being (*Wujud*), they accord a derivative, relative *wujud* to everything and see all existence as ultimately from One, God Himself.

In fact, whether the Being of God or His Attributes are the same as or other than God in Himself is a matter which has long been discussed. Some people, including very great scholars of Islam, consider *wujud al-Bari'* (oneness or unity of the Author) as the same as the Divine Being in Himself. To conclude from this that these people affirm the teaching of *wahdat al-wujud* and even of *wahdat al-mawjud* (monism) may lead one to claim that they are in error (*dalala*)—but that is a charge of such moment that we should not wish to bear the responsibility of it.

Jalal al-Din Dawwani, in his *Risalat al-Dawwani*, remarked that the being of the Real (*al-Haqq*) is the same as His Essence (*Dhat*) and that there is no real being or existent other than *Dhat al-Haqq*; and that since *wujud* is *wujud* (since "being" is precisely that which "is"), it cannot but be the being of the Real, *wujud al-Haqq*. That entails that the being of all existents is not real but *itibari* (derivative, relative). Dawwani goes a step further and observes that it is impossible to consider the creation as comprising existents that are independently, fully existent (*mustaqil*) both in their being (*wujud*) and in their outward manifestness: "Regarding *wujud*, it is impossible to attribute [independent] existence to *'alam* (the universe); it is impossible for anything to exist in itself. Regarding outward manifestness, it is impossible to attribute an independent existence to *mumkinat*, because a thing can only be manifest relatively to the Real Being, to the *Wujud* who is *al-Haqq* (the Real). No actual existent (*mustaqil haqiqa*) has its real being except in relation to Real Being, its being depends upon His Being—on that dependence it can be said to exist. Therefore, we should not consider entities that we know to be conjectural (*wahm*) and imaginary (*khayal*) as actually existent (*mawjud*)."

Ibn al-'Arabi goes still further and insists that what is visible in the universe is a manifestation and reflection, it is never a *mawjud* (existent), not even derivatively. God constantly and continually manifests Himself and the universe is constantly and continually renewed. These manifestations succeed one other and the universe constantly and continually goes back and forth between existence and non-existence because of these consecutive manifestations. These manifestations succeed one another so rapidly that no interval or gap is perceived in the continuous hierarchy of beings.

Mawlana Jalal al-Din al-Rumi shares the same views and expresses them in a colorful way: "O Soul of our souls! Who are we that dare to attribute existence to themselves? (in comparison to You, what or who are we that dare to make such a claim.) We are a large number of nothing. Our existences are nothing, either. As to You, You are the *Wujud al-Mutlaq*, who exhibits all the *fani'* (the transient, perishable entities) on a mirror in which everything is going to appear. Each of us is a lion, but one that is not real— one such as might be embroidered on a flag is moved by the blowing wind. Its movements are seen in the movements of the flag but the wind that moves them is not seen—may that Unseen never withhold His blessings from us! Our existence is bestowed by You and we are Your creation only. You made non-existence taste the flavor of existence, and made it in eternity Your enraptured (lover)." Such a view which holds everything to be the manifestation of *al-Haqq* cannot attribute being to anything. While Rumi considers that the universe does have being, that it exists, it does so figuratively (*majazi*) and because of its being a manifestation of *al-Haqq*.

Yet there is a multiplicity and variety in the visible world. Some Sufis, as we have just noted, consider this multiplicity and variety as manifestation of *al-Haqq* and explain it as dependent upon the skills (*istidat*) of the mirrors; and they hold that such a view is not contrary or harmful to the unity of Divine Being.

Junayd al-Baghdadi conveys the same view in his well-known remark: "The water takes on the color of the cup." True or Real Being is One. Just as the Light is One, for all that it illumines— all creatures are reflections and ripple-waves of this Light. Just as rain droplets, which appear in different forms, as water, ice and vapor, are different states of one substance. Similarly, things and events, which flow by and are differently manifest, are the manifestations of the same Reality.

Unlike the early Sufis whose views lead to a sound belief in *tawhid*, those of the *mutasawwifa* group who treat *wahdat al-wujud* in a philosophical way have not been able to stay clear of expressions and utterances which incline to *hulul* and *ittihad*. In fact, when they expand on the subject scientifically and philosophically, they cannot be thought free from such a consequence.

Indeed, they even seek evidence for their position in verses of the Qur'an and the hadiths of the Prophet, peace and blessings be upon him.

The verses are:

> It is not you who slew; it was God. When you threw (a handful of dust), it was not your act, but God's . . . (Anfal 8:17)

> Verily those who plight their fealty to you do no less than plight their fealty to God . . . (Fath 68:10)

> It was We who created man, and We know what dark suggestions his soul makes to him: for We are nearer to him than his jugular vein. (Qaf 50:17)

The hadiths are:

God the All-Mighty says, "O man! I was ill, but you didn't visit me." Man says, "My Lord! You are the Lord of all the realms, how can I visit You?" God says, "Do you not know that so-and-so of my servants got ill, but you did not visit him. If you had visited him, you would have found Me with him."[1]

God the All-Mighty says: ". . . My servant does not draw near to Me with anything more loved by Me than the religious duties that I have imposed upon him, and My servant continues to draw near to Me with supererogatory works so that I shall love him. When I love him, I am his hearing with which he hears, his seeing with which he sees, his hand with which he strikes, his foot with which he walks. . ."[2]

It would be possible to narrate many more such hadiths and other Qur'anic verses. However, believing that to do so would not add to the argument, we keep the discussion short. Also, the remarks on this subject of the great men of Sufism, of which we have mentioned only a few so far, are too many to ignore. However, as dealing with them fully in the scope of this question-answer would be impossible and, perhaps, unnecessary, we have limited our attention to only a few.

First of all, characterizing the first two verses quoted above among the *muhkamat* (the clear truths) of the Qur'an and thus closing the door to any contradiction of the Muslim creed, is the surest way of right interpretation to which many great *mufassirs* (interpreters of the Qur'an) have adhered.

It does not make much matter whether the action mentioned in the verse is ascribed to God or to His Prophet; either it is a miracle or an action that is attributed by God to His most glorious servant to assure his glory; or it expresses his might and power, confirming his truth.

In fact, in the above verses, what is used to justify an extreme interpretation of *wahdat al-wujud*, rather emphasizes and confirms the (separate) reality of what exists in the world. For, the difference of unbeliever and believer, of slayer and slain, and *muhatab* (third person), are mentioned: it is possible to deduce unity of being only by means of elaborate and far-fetched interpretations. Especially to deduce from ". . .*We are nearer to Him than his jugular vein,*" a meaning in favor of *wahdat al-wujud* is impossible.

In the hadiths, what is obvious is separateness and multiplicity, not unity, of being. To acknowledge that a servant (*'abd*) is a distant, secondary creature until he acquires nearness (*qurbiya*) to God, and then to talk about unity of the two is a rather crude form of belief in *hulul* and *ittihad* (in-dwelling and union) which even the *mutasawwifa* do not accept. Moreover, even in the words of the "people of God," uttered to affirm Oneness of Being, a duality is evident:

> *You are either the sun or the sea; either the Mountain Qaf or Phoenix.*
> *O Being, who is beyond the comprehension of mind!*
> *You are the Eternal and Limitless.*
> *However, since You manifest Yourself in countless chapters (forms), both*
> *those who unite with or liken themselves to You are all enraptured.*
>
> Rumi

Without needing further comment and interpretation, it is obvious that everything there said or aspired to rests on duality and multiplicity. Although other people look for evidence for *wahdat al-wujud* in the words of the *mutasawwifa*, the *mutasawwifa* themselves are always seen to affirm the realm of multiplicity by their actions, such as to annihilate their *nafs* (selfhood, carnal self). Except for the separateness from God, what is the meaning of all the hardships and disciplines of those who hold to the teaching of *wahdat al-wujud*, of their striving for perfection, their seeking to be rid of their deficiencies? Moreover, the profound sincerity in the servanthood to God of those great people absolutely contradicts the extremist, philosophical understanding of *wahdat al-wujud*.

As long as any believer in *wahdat al-wujud* accepts his own answerability to God, his servanthood to God, it means that he is acknowledging the difference of *'amir* (the superior) and *ma'mur* (the subordinate). After acknowledging subordination, to insist literally on unity of *wujud* is sheer self-contradiction. And, bar a few unbelievers who reject servanthood, no believer has ever dared to reject servanthood to God. Therefore, whereas the understanding of *wahdat al-wujud* of the *sufiyya*—which in reality concerns *wahdat al-shuhud* (the unity or oneness of witnessing)—is a result of the affective state in Sufism, *istighraq* (absorption in ecstatic contemplation, beatitude), and of a lack of words and phrases to express what they feel, the understanding of *wahdat al-wujud* of some of the *mutasawwifa* derives from the frailty and insufficiency of rendering in philosophical concepts and arguments what the Sufi experiences as inward consciousness and witnessing: moreover, these philosophical concepts and arguments have their origin less in Islam than in a school of thought developed out of a Western-Christian/Greek philosophy.

The allegation should not be accepted that, under the influence of Neo-Platonist, some great Muslims sought to introduce a doctrine of "pantheism" into Islam. The most that could be said is that those Muslims may have considered it not dangerous temporarily to borrow some terms from the Neo-Platonist since they could not find the words they needed to express what they experienced in their *mushahadat* (visions) and perceptions. Otherwise, there is a world of difference between those two groups of people in terms of their understanding of the Divine Essence.

A group of people who had found the balance of the world and the Hereafter as that balance is conveyed by the Qur'an can never be considered to agree on an understanding of *wahdat al-wujud* such as is attributed to the *mutasawwifa*:

1. A belief in One God who is everything everywhere means accepting the most unsuitable and irrelevant things to be "God," the absurdity of which any sense must reject.

2. The Qur'an adduces evidence from the universe and creation for the Oneness and Existence of God, which indicates that the reality of the created world is *thabit* (securely established).

3. In the Qur'an, many verses reiterate that the universe is going to be destroyed, after which a new world will be established. The destruction and extinction of something is meaningless unless it first exists. To talk about the destruction of something whose reality is not *thabit* is absurd and futile. And the Qur'an is altogether free from of absurdity or futility.

4. All the Prophets, peace be upon them, teach that all beings, great or small, were created second, and insistently reiterate the doctrine that the relation between God and all other existents is only a relation between the Creator and what He created. In the understanding of *wahdat al-wujud* attributed to the *mutasawwifa*, the Prophets and the truths given to them by revelation have to be declared false and denied, which is an abomination to heart and mind.

5. Every piece of evidence adduced to support a simple, literal understanding of *wahdat al-wujud*, in fact gives support to the argument for multiplicity of being.

6. A great number of verses in the Qur'an affirm that the obedient will be rewarded and the rebellious will be punished. From a literal understanding of unity of being, any judgment of this kind is an impossibility, since it would be impossible to answer such questions as, "Who is obedient?" "What is a blessing (*ni'ma*) and where is it?" "Who is guilty?" "What is punishment?" and so on.

7. If all things are accepted to be of God and events to be some sort of manifestation of Him, it would be injustice to criticize idols and the idolatrous. For, as all events are manifestations of Him, idols and the idolatrous cannot be reckoned other than Him. On the other hand, it is obvious that the Qur'an and Sunna, which establish *tawhid*, are the greatest enemy of unbelief and idolatry.

8. If *wahdat al-wujud* is accepted as the *mutasawwifa* accept it, it necessitates the idea that matter is *qadim* (eternal), which is, by the consensus of the community (*bi-l-ijma'*) tantamount to *kufr* (unbelief) and those who are truly "people of God" are absolutely far from and free of committing such a *kufr*.

There are clear differences between the *mutassawwifa* understanding of *wahdat al-wujud* and a literal-philosophical understanding of the concept which declines into pantheism. There is, to be sure, an outward similarity between the two. The philosophical understanding holds that God and the universe have the same being, a position divides into two:

1. God is a Real Being and the universe is nothing but an assemblage or arrangement or composition of some manifestations (*tazahurat*) or emanations (*sudurat*). This is a view held by Spinoza and his followers.

2. Only the universe is real. God is the *majmu'* (sum/whole) of all existents (*mawjuds*). This is the view of a naturalist pantheism sometimes associated with Hegel and his followers.

In short, the difference is this: As a result of having experienced *fana'* (extinction) the *mutasawwifa* deny the reality of the universe, the philosophical group ignore the Creator of the universe and try to put Him aside. While the *mutasawwifa* understanding of *wahdat al-wujud* implies *wahdat al-shuhud* (oneness of witnessing), the others' understanding of it inclines to *wahdat al-mawjud* (monism). The first group, unable to express their affective state (*hal*), visions (*mushahada*) and *istighraq* (absorption), resort to *mutashabihat* (metaphors, allegories) due to lack of words to express what they experience. The other group theorize the concept, and try to make a formal philosophy, a science, out of it. While the first start with God and then evaluate existents and events from this respect, the latter start to deal with the experiencing subject, thus making God dependent on the existents. While there is direct experience (*dhawq*) of God with the first, there is only theory and speculation with the latter. While the first deny and lose their selves in humility before God, the latter make the philosophy of their being like *wajib al-wujud*.

God knows best.

2.3.

How can we avoid sins, and how can we show sincere repentance?

It is very important for our spiritual and emotional life to pay special attention to repentance, the greatest shelter against sins, in the following respects:

Reaction to Sin

One's reaction to a sin that he or she has committed is closely related to one's moral and spiritual station. There may be an instance in which, because of a sin, you prostrate yourself before God and implore Him to forgive you. There may also be a case when such actions do not satisfy you, when your sorrow lights an internal fire in your heart. But we can hope that the sorrow disturbing your heart in the name of repentance may be more acceptable to God.

Repentance is indeed regret and an internal fever. In this respect, one should regard sins as being in the company of serpents and poisonous centipedes. Only such a firm attitude is acceptable from a believer, for any contrary one implies doubts about the outcomes of a sin in the Hereafter. Therefore, it is essential that every sin be confronted in an alert manner and, if committed, be succeeded by regret.

Sins Must Be Short-Lived

Since every sin engenders a new sin, whenever a person commits a sin, he or she must seek purification without delay. After all, no one knows when he or she will pass away. Those who are conscious of God cannot be at ease until they have cleansed themselves from sin. It is detrimental to a person's spiritual well-being if he or she allows a sin to survive for even one second. Moreover, such an attitude implies revering something that God does not like. Sins do not have the right to live. They must be ephemeral, because if they are not removed through repentance they become serpents constantly biting one's heart. And once the heart gets a stain, it is easier to get more. The end result is a vicious circle. Every sin engenders a new sin and at last, *Indeed, on their hearts is the stain of the (ill) that they do* (Mutaffifin 83:14) becomes evident on them.

For this reason, it is very important to remind people of these realities and alert them to sins. Moreover, if you can do so, you must reveal the ugly nature of sin to people and make them renounce their sins.

Apparently, sensitive and alert souls can smell the offensive odor that sins exude.

Sins Must Be Regarded as Detestable

When repenting, one of the most important things is to view the particular sin as something detestable and disgusting. If we do not abstain from sins, believing that they are like being with serpents and scorpions and therefore deserve our disgust, we will not have the resolve to struggle against them through repentance. When you break a priceless crystal vase, for example, you feel sorrow. In the same way, every sin you commit cracks and dirties your life lantern. Thus it is necessary to feel regret and sorrow after each sin, at least to the degree of sorrow felt after breaking a crystal vase. Otherwise, you are not taking your sins and your repentance seriously.

The Correspondence between Sin and Repentance

One's repentance for a given sin must match the sin's degree of seriousness, for every sin resembles a well filled with pitch. In other words, it is easy to fall into but very hard to get out of.

Recognizing Sin

If we belittle the outcomes of a sin, we are committing another sin equivalent to the first one. For instance, if one considers fornication or violation of another's property rights as sins exaggerated by religion and says that "we benefit from them, so why consider them sins?" he or she is committing an even bigger sin. Thus, we have to resist sins and condition ourselves in this way: "O sins, the doors of my heart are locked, so your zeal to get into my heart is in vain."

The simile of the great scholar Bediüzzaman Said Nursi is very expressive: "Run away from a sin as if it is a poisonous serpent or a centipede." Note that he likens sin to a serpent and a centipede, rather than a lion or a tiger. One can take measures before a lion or a tiger attacks, for they attack bravely, whereas a serpent and a centipede attacks unexpectedly and maliciously. Backstabbing and treachery may be considered examples of such sins.

In short, vigilance against sins must be an attribute of a true believer. We have to keep in mind that vigilance against sins is an indication of our loyalty and fidelity to our Lord, the Almighty.

To realize the true nature of sins, we can look from the point of view of holy saying of Prophet Muhammad: "Adhnaba 'abdi dhanban,"[3] which is about a servant of God who sins and then repents. In this saying, the words used have a very deep meaning: dhanb (sin) and dhanab (tail) come from the same root in Arabic. Thus, a believer who says: "O my Lord, I have committed a sin," means to say: "O my Lord, I have put on a tail again. In my present state, You may consider me a fox with a furry tail, a scorpion stinging others with its tail, or a serpent whose tail is a long part of its body! And that is me!" In other words, those who confess their sins in reality confess that they have scorned and belittled the humanity granted to them by God and, as a result, have fallen to the level of the animals.

As for the one who sins and is unaware of it, he or she is a mirror of the verse: *They are like cattle, or rather are even more misguided* (7:179) and has fallen to a level below the animals.

CHAPTER 3

Virtues and Hardships
in the Service of Islam

3.1.

How can "moderation" be defined?

Moderation is the balanced way between extremes, the middle way between two excesses: *ifrat* (too much) and *tafrit* (too little). It is also to use one's primordial nature, capacity, and skills to do good, to do exactly what is prescribed by the Creator, on His way. Man's faculties of sense and mind, his emotions, fear, anger and bodily desire, and the like, are innate in him and play a major role in his life. If these gifts are well used as they were meant to be used, moderation is achieved. On the other hand, insufficient or excessive use of them bring about deviations.

For example: bodily desire is, in general terms, a desire to obtain whatever is a means to keep people alive and their generation continuing. Eating, drinking, and such similar acts are also parts of bodily desire, which sustain physical existence and health. To abstain altogether from such desire, as some Christian nuns and monks do to achieve perfection of will, is *tafrit*: it is a form of excess, an excess of omission and abstinence. On the other hand, to accept no boundaries and to consider everything permissible is *ifrat*, another form of excess, arrogant indulgence. The clear way between the extremes of self-denial and self-indulgence is self-discipline:

The emotion of anger is also a gift to humankind made for particular reasons. It too must be applied in correct measure. For instance, to cause great damage to oneself and others in order to avenge a trifle, ruthlessly to shed blood, this is *ifrat*. On the other hand, to be silent and abstain from anger against gross injustice, against violation of one's honor, or against the dishonoring of the sacred things, is *tafrit*. Moderation lies in the middle path. It is to raise your voice against injustice, tyranny and oppression, and to be firm and implacable against them, but to be soft-hearted and compassionate to the weak and innocent, and to be patient if, for that situation, patience brings about good.

Excessive worry or groundless fear, being afraid of every thing—possible accidents, thunder-storms, superstitions or anything in the universe—make life unbearable for the one who suffers them, and this is *ifrat*. The banks of the Ganges are lined with examples of people who attribute divinity to many things and forces in nature which they fear and to which they plead for help in the form of idols which are as helpless themselves. However, being totally fearless and having no cares or worries about anything, on earth or in the heavens, when one is normally expected to fear and worry, this is *tafrit*. This is probably a sort of insanity in which doing harm to oneself and endangering the lives of those close by is inevitable. Moderation is to take some precautionary measures to protect one's life and the lives of those close to one, and not to attach too much importance to far-fetched worries and ill-defined probabilities.

The terms *ifrat, tafrit* and moderation apply also to reason. Without taking the outcomes of observation and perception into account, to depend only on reason is *ifrat*. This is what the sophists or logicians of ancient times did in their games of wit or what today's materialists do in their dialectics. Denial of reason altogether, rejection of all mental phenomena and categories of mind, relying instead on either a bare, external positivism or an intuitive, subjective consciousness as the only truth—this is *tafrit*. Examples of this are the positivism of Comte and certain sorts of mysticism in Christianity. Moderation in reasoning and thinking is to compose and then reach new ideas through the evaluation of the input of subjective feeling and objective observation. In this way, one can comprehend what is not within the limits of either intuition alone or observation alone. Straightforwardness in the use of mind can only be achieved through the guidance of Divine Revelation. Otherwise, the mind when it turns away from the Divine Revelation is nothing but self-willed craft and obstinacy mixed with pride.

Moderation, as we have said, is one of the essentials in all the faculties and senses that we are endowed with. The same is true of the obligations and duties laid upon us, and in respect of sound belief. Disbelief in the existence of God and rejection of His Attributes is atheism. On the other hand, accepting that He has a material being or form, or attributing to Him a location or human qualities, is also unbelief. The middle way between these two extremes is that, when one believes in the existence of God, one acknowledges that He is One, the Creator, and that He is free from fault, want and need, and that His Attributes are perfect and Divine.

All the other matters related to faith can be dealt with in the same way. For instance, believing that humankind has no will and no power is predestination as compulsion. Believing that humankind is the doer and creator of all their acts and handiwork is extreme voluntarism. The middle way is to acknowledge that humankind has free will as an ordinary condition and that God alone creates everything. Moderation is the true practice (*'amal*), too. If the sensual and carnal life in this world make us forget or ignore spirituality and the Hereafter, this is materialism, which is *ifrat*. Mystical spiritualism which totally denies sensuous bodily existence is *tafrit*. The balanced view between these extremes is to deal with everything in accordance with the balance between body and soul, between this world and the Hereafter. This kind of faith is genuine and it is itself moderation.

In the light of this argument, we can argue that some world religions display examples of extremism on both ends. The only right response for a murder in a religion can be death penalty, without any chance of forgiveness; whereas another religion would impose no sanction on the murderer or fail to observe justice by only prescribing to forgiveness only, and nothing else. Islam achieves moderation by taking the middle path, establishing the principle of "measure for measure" but with the door always open to forgiveness. When we look at any aspect of life, whether it be theoretical or practical, we shall clearly see that Islam commands, and is, the way of moderation in every case.

Social moderation which is bound to concern every people constituted as a society is an unattainable ideal unless the members of that society have attained a sufficient level of straightforwardness in their thinking and practical life and in their economic relationships. That straightness of conduct, in turn, cannot be sustained unless and until a sufficient number of people in that society understand, desire and practice the virtue of moderation.

3.2.

How should people avoid sins, distractions, and temptations?

T he question refers to one of the greatest difficulties of modern life. Even the not-so-young, but of course especially the young live in a social environment that exaggerates the natural pressures of youth to an extreme; ever-present temptations and passing desires scatter one's nobler sentiments and higher aspirations. It is difficult indeed in this environment to represent the sublime qualities of person and character that the Messenger of God exemplified and willed his followers to emulate; but, to live at such a time and to struggle against the desires and temptations has its own particular advantages. This is because the reward of all effort is proportionate to the hardship of the conditions endured.

Is it not the hardship of the struggle he endured which earned Hamza the titles "the master of the martyrs" and "the lion of God"? His battle-cry to his men—"The enemies are many, but we have faith," and charging the enemy front-line with self-sacrificing disregard for death—these are the qualities that raised him to such a high rank.

When Islam was first preached, the women among the idolaters used to circumambulate the Ka'ba naked; adultery, fornication, usury, profiteering, exploitation, bribery, drinking and gambling were deeply embedded in the manners of the society.

And yet, the Companions turned their backs on such practices and embraced Islam. They were all normal human beings with feelings and appetites like all others. But their giving up and leaving aside carnal desires and immoral practices in that environment, their preferring a pure and honest way of life, and their support of the revived, true religion and the Messenger who preached it—and their doing so, despite all dangers, threats and persecutions, made them nobler than the rest and greater than all the greats. By doing so, they gained such merits and virtues that they have become the light and, like the stars in the heavens, guide those who come after them.

The kinds of obstacles, disasters and destructions they faced exist also today. In a spiritual assembly, Bediüzzaman Said Nursi was named as the man of the age of disasters and destruction.[1] If the Prophet called the people who try to live and serve Islam sincerely in this age, he would definitely name them as the generation of the age of disasters and destruction. For, if the streets and market-places, city centers, social and commercial business, individual and family life, schools (which nurture the rest) and all other societal entities and institutions which together make up collective life and its norms—if these were assessed one by one, the verdict on each of them would be "bad, spoiled or ruined."

Wherever you go, you cannot avoid some or other sort of foulness or sin staining your senses; the atmosphere is invasive, aggressive. To do or finish a job in the community, you cannot pass from one side to the other without your soul and heart being assaulted and your spiritual life shaken. To live Islam is as hard as walking on a road of fire or going across a river of foul blood. We are creatures of such a time of disasters and destruction. The sensuality, carnality, corporeality hidden in the self is like the tail of a scorpion lifted and ready to strike. Those appetites and lusts always feed upon and grow in the conditions prevalent (and systematically encouraged) in this modern society. It is possible to be poisoned at any instant by the scorpions within and around us. We must be aware of the conditions and evaluate them in the light of "the reward is proportionate to the hardship endured," and so feel somewhat lightened and encouraged by the hope of a recompense whose magnitude will reflect the hardship and affliction we have overcome. The more successful we are in defeating the enemies, the more we will be rewarded. If the Companions acquired their high rank by overcoming the hardships and afflictions they faced, then people today could do and achieve almost as much in a similar way— which is what we expect from the Divine Mercy. Today, when the conditions for committing sins are so easy, of course there must have been some errors and sins of ours that we committed unintentionally; but it behooves us, and we need, not to leave the gate of Divine Mercy; rather, we must be persistent there. Let me tell you one of my childhood memories, which reflects how I think and feel. When I was a child we had a very faithful dog which guarded our flocks of sheep. I so admired its loyalty that I fed it frequently and even sometimes played with it. When I raised my little hands in prayer, I remembered the significance of its loyalty to us and put it next to my hopes and prayed to God: "O my Lord, just as I treated that dog as a friend on account of its loyalty to us, so forgive me, such a slave of Yours, who has never left You and the gates of Your Divine Mercy and who has never prayed and bowed before anyone else but You."

The same is true for Muslims (who have never left Him and the gates of His Divine Mercy and who have never prayed and bowed before anyone else but He). In spite of some slips, mistakes and sins, there are such Muslims who serve in the way of God so sincerely and faithfully that God, the Most Merciful, will not drive them from the gates of His Mercy. We accept and admit our faults. Such admissions, confessions, are a part of journeying through regrets, remorse and repentance. We ask Him again and again to forgive our wrong-doings out of His Mercy, in accordance with His Grace. And God accepts and answers such prayers done wholeheartedly, with faith and sincerity.

What we have said so far was by way of reporting the situation we are in. Let us now look briefly at some points about what to do and how to act.

- I -

On slippery, dangerous roads, one walks very carefully, as if through a mine field or dangerous enemy territory. A comparable caution and alertness are necessary while one goes out in the streets and market-places, because it is always possible that the forbidden things will present themselves to our eyes. One should avoid looking at and seeing the forbidden by casting down the eyes or turning the face away. One who shuts his eyes to the forbidden does not lose anything materially and spiritually, and he does not give any harm to anybody. One who works efficiently, honestly and sincerely and serves in the way of God, can never be a passive victim of evil and vice. On the other hand, those who stare at others or let others stare at them do not gain anything thereby except danger. Hospitals, courts, prisons and the reports in the dailies are clear testimony of what such persons themselves, who court danger, and their partners, families, societies and countries, have lost by doing so. You cannot expect much from those who paralyzed their hearts and wills by wandering glances.

In one hadith the Prophet said: "A time will come when to preserve faith will be like holding a red hot cinder in one's palms. If you throw it away, you will lose your faith, if you keep it, you will get burnt."[2]

In another hadith he said: "*Nazar* (glancing at the forbidden) is one of the poisonous arrows of Satan."[3] When it hits the heart or penetrates it through the channel of the eyes, one perishes. And the Prophet expressed the Divine Will in his words and added that: "If anyone leaves it out of fear of Me, I will give his heart such an exhilaration of faith that he feels it thoroughly in the very depths of his heart."[4]

The Prophet expressed his attitude toward the poisonous arrows of Satan in speech and also demonstrated it in his dealings with his close relatives. While they were descending from Mount

Arafat during the pilgrimage, he let his cousin, Fadl, son of 'Abbas, ride on his camel. In order to prevent his cousin's gaze being caught by the women who were passing by them, the Prophet with his hand pushed his cousin's head from one side to the other.[5] Recall that this happened during pilgrimage, when any intention to look at women for pleasure is impossible, and when, in the words of 'Aisha, mother of believers, women used to cover even their faces, at a time when everyone felt the sublime atmosphere of the Archangel Gabriel's Revelations, the nearness of the Hereafter, and the miracles, the Age of Happiness. Even as we seek to control our hearts in the mosques and in the company of other sincere Muslims, how should we evaluate the Prophet's turning his cousin's face from one side to another during a Hajj in that epoch? The Prophet did so because he did not want his cousin to be distracted, to be hit by a poisonous arrow which might sow the seeds of evil and vice in his heart and mind, even at a time when Fadl was far from dreaming of such a thing.

The meaning of this event is to cut off evil at its root. It is like not allowing a box of matches into the forest so as to protect it from being burnt down; or, even when there is no threat of war, to maintain the practice of guarding the frontiers and headquarters with many sentries; or to stuff all the holes and crevices so that snakes and scorpions have no dwelling-places in which to breed. That is, to set barriers before vice and evil so as to prevent many individuals from being led astray and families broken; to eliminate all the ways and means leading to rape, adultery, murder, all sorts of immorality, perversions and corruptions; and to deter all sins by prevention. That is the way defined by God.

The Prophet said to 'Ali, who became a Muslim at the age of seven, who grew up within the atmosphere of the Prophet, was his cousin and was to be the father of the generations that would come from the Prophet's lineage: "O 'Ali, the first glance is in your favor, but the second is against you." That is, when your eye lights on something forbidden, you will not be responsible for that glance because it is unintentional and accidental. Your will is not in that first look. But, if you do not turn your eyes from it and keep on looking, your carnal self and will are in it, and you will be questioned and punished for it; because this is the first ring of a chain that will drag you into deviation, into the forbidden. So the Prophet would have us close the gates to the forbidden, to prevent it in advance, before it can happen.

- II -

One should not go out simply when one is bored. Going out just out of boredom is a weakness and error of attitude. For, one exposes oneself thereby to more negatives, a sort of "falling out of the frying pan into the fire."

Boredom arises from the dissatisfaction of the heart, lack of closeness and relation to the Prophet and God, being unable to do the religious duties and prayers properly or adequately, being free or idle due to not reading and contemplating enough, having few good friends and having no duty or responsibility on one's shoulders to fulfill or not serving in the way of God as one is supposed to. In such a person, there are many openings for Satan to get into. This is like walking again through the trenches where one was wounded by Satan, or like drinking sea-water to quench a thirst aroused by drinking sea-water.

There is another way to look at this situation. God, in virtue of His name *Qabdh*, grips man's heart and puts him into a state of *qabdh* (literally, "contraction," "gripping"); a state of spiritual desolation, which is a test for man to see his level of determination and loyalty. That is, the man is tested to see whether he will turn to God and do prayers and supplications—or turn away. Let me point out here that prayers, supplications, duties and services done in such a state are far more rewarding than those done at *bast* (literally, "expansion," "extension"), in a joyful and happy state, or than those done with ease, amid other Muslims at normal times of congregation. And later on, as the sun shines after a short burst of cloudy weather, God, in virtue of His name *Basit*, expands the man's heart and returns him to comfort and eagerness. Thus, God gives man the reward proportionately to the hardship he endures.

In sum, one should not go out unnecessarily and, when he does so, he should try to accomplish not a single but a couple of tasks on one occasion. He should keep away from the places and districts where sins are committed and where there is no service in the way of God.

When one goes out, one should give the time and place the attention that is their due. The Companions of the Prophet, like Abu Bakr, 'Umar and Abu Dhar, often went out to teach the truths of Islam. Those who go out onto the public streets with such aims in mind give the streets their due right and thus are protected from committing sins. When the Prophet forbade his Companions to sit alongside the roadway, they said they had some business or good reason for doing so. Then the Prophet said: "Then give the roadway its due," that is, clean it of all stones, thorns or obstacles, receive and respond to the greetings of passers-by, enjoin the good and forbid the bad and tell them the truths. Only with this pure intention, one's sins and wrong-doings can be replaced and turn to good deeds.

- III -

One should refer to, read, listen to, or have to do with works that encourage knowledge, awe and fearful reverence (*makhafa*), purify the senses and feelings, direct one's attention to the higher purpose of living in this world, and keep one's thoughts and feelings under the influence of that purpose while one is going out to school, or work, or is engaged in service. One should review one's purpose before going out, take a deep look at the self's accounts and balance-sheet, do self-supervision, and be equipped with some spiritual tension so that it may serve as a cover, or shield, between oneself and vice. In that way one may be protected by God from Satan and sins.

- IV -

One should not go out, as it were, unattended. One should have the company of one or more good friends who can always help guide one's attention and who are accessible for consultation and who can keep one's spiritual resources alert through guidance and counseling. For, often one's inner control may not suffice to brake and hold oneself safe against temptations. One's level of faith may not be of the strength and quality to feel that one is always under the watchful supervision of God. One may sometimes suffer such weak moments that self-control fails, one's gaze slips to the forbidden, and thus one receives a wound in the soul, the seed of bad ideas may spread in the mind and a sin begin to ferment in the soul. However, when one has good friends around, each watching out for the others, conversation can always turn to good things and one can be more careful about what enters the eyes and ears. There are moments when one will forget that the watchful supervision of God is constant; in such moments, the desire and need not to embarrass and disgrace one's friends may serve to prevent acts or manners that constitute or lead to wrong-doing. This may be considered a lack of sincerity, to some extent even a sort of hypocrisy, a mere pretending to be good; but, whereas hypocrisy ruins the essence of the positive deeds, like *salat* (prescribed daily prayers), it does not ruin the negative deeds, the not-doing of what is bad. For example, if a man does not commit adultery while only pretending to be good, still he did not commit that sin, or if he does not steal something only because people are watching him, even so he did not steal. When the adultery of the hand or foot, eye or ear, or mind, or whatever else will draw man's imagination toward sin is renounced, even to seem good to others, one is considered to be safe from that sin unless and until it takes control of the soul and one commits the sin, as it were, in the heart though not daring to do it in fact. Furthermore, there is some reward in not committing and renouncing the forbidden. For instance, each closing of the eyes to the forbidden earns man the reward of a *wajib* (necessary) act.

- V -

While coming, going or staying somewhere else one should, to the extent practicable, carry with him the works and materials related to our world of faith and religion. These will serve to protect him, like guarding angels. These materials, which act as a shield against sins, will be the means for inward contemplation, for watchful supervision. A person who is accompanied or surrounded by such materials can commit sins only with difficulty.

- VI -

As soon as one has done something wrong, one should repent and turn to the Divine forgiveness. Sin is going out of the atmosphere of God's favor, Grace, and denial of His security. In each sin, there is always a way leading to new sins. One who has committed a sin already becomes an easier target for Satan, more likely to be targeted again and commit that sin again. As one's sins increase, God's security and protection against them decrease.

The place where a sin is least able to dwell is the believer's heart. The wrongs should be transient there, like passing clouds on a sunny day, and should fade quickly. Sin is foulness, a stain, rust. As it is expressed in a hadith, when foulness and rust pile up because not cleaned off immediately, they come in between the heart and God, cut off the manifestations coming from Him, hinder the winds of His Mercy and deprive one of His Grace. Could there be an easier target for Satan to hit than such a heart?

No matter what the nature of the sin, one should never permit such a negative effect to build up in the heart and soul. Therefore, turn to God, express remorse, repent, ask for His forgiveness, take refuge in His infinite Grace and Mercy. One of the Companions came to the Prophet very upset, and said that he was utterly perished. He explained that on the way he had looked at a woman or touched her. He was so remorseful, indeed devastated, on account of his sin that God sent Gabriel with the following verse:

> And establish regular prayers at the two ends of the day [fajr, zuhr, 'asr] and at the approaches of the night [magrib, isha]. For those things that are good remove those that are evil. That is a reminder for the mindful. (Hud 11:114)

It is by the prayers that we keep away from evil, and God forgives the sins and replaces them with good. In particular, waking up for the *tahajjud* (a very rewarding supererogatory prayer observed in the night), which is the light of the intermediate world, leaving the comfort of bed and sleep during the latter hours of the night, and turning to God in prayer—is a sure means of undoing mistakes and cleansing the stain of sins quickly.[6]

Prayers and supplications in the late hours of the night done by a heart full of fear and hope will certainly be accepted by God, provided that they are from the heart with sincerity. To do the five daily prayers at the appointed times of worship, each of which signifies the milestones of a day in humanity's life, are a means for any wrong-doings and sins committed between two times of prayer to be forgiven.[7] More than that, we should also try to earn God's pleasure by supererogatory prayers, especially the *tahajjud*.[8]

A separate but important issue is that one who has committed a crime that embarrasses him will not want anyone to become aware of it. However, he is totally aware that God and His Angels saw and know what he did. Satan lies in wait for just such an eventuality and will seek to make the sinner say: "I wish there were none who saw and knew about my sin," or even "I wish it were not a sin"—Remember that not accepting as a sin what God has forbidden leads to unbelief.

Insistence on committing a sin and considering it trivial may also lead one to unbelief. Some people may be so habituated to sins they cannot extricate themselves. It can happen that we unintentionally push such people into far worse situations in an effort to rescue them. For example, if we say to a weak Muslim, "Don't drink. It is forbidden," he may respond: "A little or a cupful cannot be forbidden," or "I find the rule too strict." Likewise, in response to insistent words calling to *salat*, a weak individual may respond with: "I'm not coming." Such responses belong to unbelief, so the individual may be led astray.

Essentially, sin is sin when it is insisted on, considered trivial, not feared for its harm, not repented, and for which forgiveness is not asked. Otherwise, if one is not persisting in a sin, knows the harm and damage of it, tries to shun it, repents the doing of it, and seeks forgiveness, by the grace of God, as the Qur'an states, one will be granted forgiveness and mercy. Though the sin be the size of a mountain, one should not despair, for there is no sin that God will not forgive, except the sin of *shirk* (associating partners with God)—and one who commits that will not turn to God for forgiveness; he will seek solace (if at all) at the court of some false or non-existent power.

- VII -

One should not be free or idle, and should take on some duties, responsibilities and services on him. Satan makes use of idleness and inactivity, and does not like one's being enlightened intellectually and spiritually so as to live and serve in the way of God. If one is empty of responsibility, then Satan preoccupies the mind and heart with fantasies, sins, and forbidden things. One can block up all the holes through which Satan leaks into the mind and heart by energetic activity and tries to prevent serving in the way of God. One who runs to spread the message of God to others without stopping to rest and congratulate himself will feel energy, vitality, and joy in both body and soul. As is stated in a hadith, since one enjoins the good and forbids the wrong, he will feel the blessings and inspirations of the Divine Revelations in his life, his food and necessities of life will be blessed and abundant, and his home (family) will be one of the abodes of Paradise. As is further pointed out in the hadith, if such duty and service in the way of God, is forsaken, this blessings of the Revelations will be cut off, and those who are deprived of such blessings will be doomed and perish in darkness and afflictions.

- VIII -

God will help and protect those who dedicate themselves to God, Islam, the Prophet, the communicating the Truth and the awakening or the enlightenment of people. God Himself makes a covenant with such people:

> O You who believe, if you help [the cause of] God, He will help you, and plant your feet firmly. (Muhammad 47:7)

So it is obvious that God will not let those people be deviated, corrupted and caused to perish by any sort of evil or vice, or Satanic selfhood. The Prophet said that if someone draws near to God, God will draw near to him tenfold, if someone walks to God, God will run to him. So if one acts upon Islam, performs the prayers and obligations, and helps the Cause of God, he will be rewarded manifold, and God will not let him be distracted, deceived, or led astray by desires and temptations, his sins will be replaced by good and righteous deeds, and he will be recompensed with unknown, unforeseen rewards and eternal bliss.

On the one hand, we are in a terrible situation, surrounded by sins. On the other, we are in a situation that offers advantages that make up for its terrible side. With this attitude, to some extent comparable to that of the Companions, we have the opportunity of getting closer to the Companions. They could feel the breath of the Revelation on their faces, whereas we live ages apart from them. Yet, if we are able to take our place behind them with a Muhammadi spirit, we will, in one respect have assured our salvation by the grace of God.

May God not disappoint us in that hope! Amin.

3.3.

How should believers invite others to faith?

The aim of sending the Prophets is communicating the divine message, which is the most important and vital obligation incumbent on humanity. That is to say, to enlighten others with knowledge of the true religion and the duties that accompany it. In the light of this our primary duty is to review all existing and past methods and approaches, and to put into practice today those principles which it is possible to apply, and which lead to the best results. Everyone who is considered old enough to be responsible for his actions may and should serve to convey the message of God to everyone, in the recognized ways, with the courtesies proper to the task. Whatever their ages and status are, each and every individual is obliged to tell others what he is supposed to tell, and this constitutes a most vital duty. The purpose of our existence is the same too. For, God says: *I created man and jinn for no other purpose than to worship Me only* (Dhariyat 51:56). Such worship or servanthood to God is like a race, and every person will take part in it. Some will not cope with the hurdles and be detained, and some will always win and attain the furthest places in this race, even to the presence of God.

To know God and devote oneself to Him is the purpose of one's nature and the essence of creation. Devotion, servanthood, to God requires not only listening, understanding, accepting, abiding by and applying certain rules in one's life; it also means seeking the purity in ideas and mind, and striving toward the horizon of thinking of only the Creator, whose effort is a heavy, sublime, and sacred duty.

> O you people, worship your Guardian Lord Who created you and those who came before you that you may become righteous, Who has made the earth your couch, and the heavens your canopy; and sent down rain from the heavens; and brought forth therewith fruits for your sustenance; then set not up rivals unto God when you know the truth. (Baqara 2:21)

Worship your God. For He is the Creator. The Creator of you and the people who lived before you. The act of creating and the things created belong to Him alone. It is God Who brought you into existence, and Who created, in one sense, before your birth, the elements and particles which would constitute you, and Who created, in another sense, the people who came before you. It is God Who caused to perish many before you, like Pharaoh, Nimrod, Shaddad, and such. By His laws of creation, He turned the Romans, the Greeks, the Byzantines, the Ottomans and the rest, who strutted and swaggered about the earth, into ruins. So it is God Who created and caused to perish all those. Therefore, beware and worship God alone, the Almighty, the Creator, the Sustainer, and keep always in mind and before your eyes the example, lesson and warning of the past and present, so that you may enter into the circle of piety, consciousness of God.[9]

It is the Sustainer, the Almighty, who made the earth your couch, a resting place.[10] He created and provided for it in such a way that everything of need is placed within the reach of your hand. It is as if the world were a big mansion and the Owner of this mansion, the Sovereign of all the worlds, was entertaining His weak and unable guest with a great show of honor, treating him with marks of respect and distinction. If the slightest failure occurred in this couch, the guest could do nothing and would have nowhere to flee to. So everything is maintained according to the guest's wants, needs and weaknesses. When this guest lies down on his back and looks at the canopy over his head, he will see it ornamented with stars and systems for his observation. It is God Who made this magnificent canopy over His guest's couch.

He has made the heavens as a canopy well guarded.[11] There is a continual preordained coordination between the heavens and the earth. The heavens give light and heat, and the earth responds with buds and flowers; the earth returns the evaporation to the heavens, and the heavens turn it back as rainfall; the heavens have the thunders, lightning, and the earth gets its share from their fertile effects; the heavens give rain, and the earth preserves and presents it as drinking water, the living things live their lives and die, and the earth is purified and sterilized by the change of time, seasons, and so on and so forth. So we see that this guest-house is created; not left to run itself but, on the contrary, it is cared for, sustained, and provides for the guests fruits and blessings of all kinds. Therefore, turn to your Sustainer, Cherisher, Lord of all the realms, and worship Him.

We are surrounded by such magnificent order, harmony, splendor, and blessings, operated with great wisdom and power. It is apparent that light for our eyes, taste for our tongues and sound for our ears, that is, our physical and spiritual needs, are all regulated and provided, as sustenance for us. All these come from God. He is never confused while granting all these diverse kind of sustenance; and He neither needs others' help nor lets them interfere with His work. Therefore, be fair and reasonable; and do not confuse, do not associate, others in your worship of God. Avoid and save yourself from the different kinds of the ugliness of *shirk* (attributing partners to God) whether open or hidden, big or small.

All causes are accidental, secondary, none has true substance or primary reality. Had God not assigned to us recourse to causes, we would not have felt any need to refer to cause and would have regarded any attempt of that kind as *shirk*. However, since this world is the abode of wisdom and everything comes into this place entangled in causes, we just consider them as mediating conditions. But the real focus is the Giver, Creator, Who holds all causes under His disposal, therefore we worship Him alone. While attributing some share to causes, whether in the face of misfortunes, calamities and sufferings, or of joy, pleasure or delight, one should always preserve the balance, and avoid words and acts which give any hint of *shirk*. And the sensitivity to be observed on this matter is directly proportional to one's closeness to God. When one has tasted the blessing of the immaterial and spiritual pleasures, one should continue to act and worship God in a way worthy of such blessings. One should not let oneself go astray even for an instant by any inclination that might turn one to any other than God. If such an inclination occurs to one, one should come to oneself and affirm the *tawhid* and proclaim the oneness of God. Such servanthood to God done in this consciousness is the purpose of life, and every understanding of service that leads to such a purpose is an obligation, which is the wisdom in sending the prophets to carry out this obligation. So we, the believers, undertake such a sacred duty, and serving God in this way is a competition in virtue, and the people who take part are the most virtuous people of all.

If all the ways which lead to presidency were opened and the position were offered to someone who attaches importance to serving God as explained above, and if he had to choose between one or the other, the presidency or the service of God, he would certainly prefer the latter. For, he knows that this is the job which belongs to the Prophets and the truthful. In this way, there are Abu Bakr, 'Umar, 'Uthman, 'Ali and the rest, who were pure, saintly and enlightened men. On the other side are people of whom a great majority are oppressors and tyrants; their actions belong to those who have not been adequately nourished morally and spiritually, and have to do with dirty politicking, hatred, intrigue and plots.

We live such a life that neither our coming into nor going out of it is in our hands. But, it is possible for us to turn our lives from ones in which we exist and do nothing but wait for the inevitable end, to ones in which we live and make gradual progress to the level that God is pleased with us. This could be done first by digesting all the principles of faith into our souls, making them an integral part of our souls, and filling our consciences with knowledge of God; and next, aspiring to the consciousness of *ihsan*—worshipping as if we were seeing God—by raising our faith toward the level of perfect sincerity by means of constant worship, and thus making the pillars of Islam a faculty inherent in our particular nature; and finally conveying these merits, virtues and qualities, which we acquired for ourselves in the first instance, to the community, making them prevalent in all walks of life and thus enlightening all people and places.

In reflecting how to perform the duty of guidance and teaching faith, a number of points are worth bearing in mind. To set the matter out somewhat systematically can be useful in terms of giving people ideas about how to do it, but it can be harmful in terms of over-fixing and over-defining what needs to be natural and flexible. Bearing in mind the need for naturalness and flexibility, we can look briefly at a number of points.

- I -

One should seek and find ways to win entry into the heart and soul of the person addressed. There are many humane ways one may resort to, such as giving gifts or easing the person's difficulties. In fact these are ways of kindness that are an essential part of the religion, part of what we are commanded to practice when approaching people. So, first, the person we address should be in a state willing to accept our friendship, cordiality and intimacy. These are important factors if what we say is to be welcomed by that person. Therefore, every effective way legitimate and permissible in Islam should be used to win the person's heart.

- II -

We should know very well the level of faith, knowledge and culture of the person being addressed. In this way we may avoid saying or doing something that could so frighten off that person that he may never again come close to us or Islam. For example, if we open and read any Islamic publication or the Qur'an to that person, and if our doing so puts him further off from Islam, then it would be better not to read something, even the Qur'an, to him. Any material we refer to might indeed be full of inspirations which should conquer the hearts and souls of people. However, to offer such material to one who is not yet ready to welcome it, is indirectly (and unintentionally) to betray the cause of Islam.

God provides colostrum, a milk-like liquid secreted for a few days after childbirth that is high in antibody content. Later it turns to whole milk and even the content of it gradually changes as the baby grows up. This law of nature is certainly true of spiritual education and moral nourishment, too. What God manifests to us in His laws of creation should be investigated, minutely, and we should adjust our acts in accordance with them. Sometimes, as this adjustment was lacking, what was said with the intent of guidance caused such a reaction that, even if you happen to find a suitable moment to tell it again, it is ineffectual. So first of all, we should determine the level of perception, knowledge and understanding of the person, so that, as Said Nursi puts it, we do not end up offering grass to the lion and meat to the horse.[12]

- III -

Gaining the trust and respect of the person spoken to is essential. He must trust and become attached to you in such a way that you and his love for you weigh heavier than that of his other friends; because your friendship, relationship and love for that person is different from the others' and only for the sake of God, it will definitely show its effects on his heart. When he is to make a choice, he should be ready to prefer the strenuous duties the religion lays upon us, to the comfort and pleasures of the other side. Even the hardship, trouble and dangers he might experience in the way you are going should be dearer to him than the pleasures and comfort of his previous life. This can only happen for that person if he knows and trusts and loves you thoroughly.

Here is a striking and a concrete example from the Age of Happiness. Utba ibn Walid was one of the richest and the most inveterate enemies of Islam in Makka. For this reason he was given a nickname meaning, the most wretched evil-doer of his tribe. He was the head of much mischief. However, there was a fortunate person who was brought up in his house and was not like him at all. This was his son, Hudayfa, who attached himself to the Prophet loyally and rejected the most attractive things, in the worldly sense, presented and proposed to him by his father and family. What he was asked by his family was to abandon the Prophet and the cause he propagated. However, due to the lessons he took from his teacher and guide, Hudayfa's spiritual tension was exact, and his faith and conviction were firm, and he did not give in. What did the Prophet respond to such an offer made by the chieftains in Makka? "If you put the sun in my right hand and the moon in my left on condition that I abandon this course, before He has made it victorious, or I have perished therein, I would not abandon it."[13] The words the Prophet had said made such an impression in the hearts and consciences of the people that not only Hudayfa but also all the Companions would give the same answer. As a guide and teacher, the Prophet won the hearts of people in such a way that wherever and whenever his name was mentioned the effect and decrees of parents, brothers, other kith and kin, were of no avail, and only he remained as the focus of values.

From past to the present nothing much has changed in respect of the relation between the spiritual guide and the one guided. Only the time and the people change, the rest remains the same. Therefore, would-be guides and teachers should apply the Prophet's way to win the hearts of people. Otherwise, what is said will remain in the air (be ineffective) and will not meet with a friendly welcome. It is a question of reaching, penetrating and settling in the hearts of people. We must remember that if the Prophet had not made himself so loved by his Companions, they would not have gone to Badr behind him. For this was the first battle—all the conditions were completely against them; moreover, the majority of the enemies were their own sons, brothers, fathers, uncles or other relatives. However, the believers got the signal to go forward from the Prophet and believed that it was better for them to die in his way than to live with the falsehood of their kith and kin.

Sometimes the Prophet inculcated in the believers the consciousness of preferring God and His Messenger. We see in the example of Ka'b ibn Malik who failed to march out with the army to Tabuk. Ka'b himself told the story. The Prophet admonished him: "Didn't you promise to me in 'Aqaba that you would go wherever I go?" He replied: "O Messenger of God! If I were dealing with a worldly man, I am sure I would escape his displeasure through seemingly reasonable excuses, for God has endowed me with the gift of the tongue. But in your case I am sure that if I appease you with a false statement, God would be displeased with me. And, on the other hand, I am sure that if I displease you by confessing the simple truth, then God would very soon blow away your displeasure. I therefore make bold to speak the very truth. By God, I had no excuse at all. I had never been so well as I was at that time." His speaking the truth and perseverance in seeking forgiveness of God brought his salvation.[14]

The guide should enter the heart of the person he is dealing with in such a way that he can persuade him to do what he tells him; but that which he tells the other to do should not, must not, be for his carnal self. According to the Qur'an, Pharaoh, Nimrod and Shaddad represent the state of those who require from others for themselves. By contrast, the Prophets made their demands only on behalf of God or their community. This is a very subtle point and those who communicate the divine message and be a spiritual guide should pay the closest attention to it.

- IV -

We should have a sound grasp of Islam and Islamic tradition. One should not speak out whatever comes into his mind or speculate. The Prophet said that he left to us two resources, which we must adhere to, and which would allow us to differentiate light from darkness, right from wrong, namely the Qur'an and Sunna.[15] Therefore, when something is presented on behalf of the cause of Islam, it should be done within the principles of these two sources, and one should have mastered the issues being addressed. One should be well-versed, skilled and proficient in Islamic matters. One should never indulge in dialectics merely to silence the other by argumentation. What we say should be what we ourselves in the first place have understood and digested fully, so that the person we are dealing with can easily take it in and be (spiritually) nourished thereby. Just as in the analogy Bediüzzaman gave, a spiritual guide should be like a sheep, which takes in, digests and turns food into milk. So we should feed people with the most restorative, wholesome food, but should not be like a bird, which half-eats, then gives its chicks the regurgitated food.[16] If we do it the right way, we can appeal to people's minds and souls, and, considering the true knowledge and wisdom which would lead to God, and bring about the best, desired effects.

Naturally this can only be done by reading and studying, improving one's level of knowledge and culture. That is why those who assume the duty of communicating the divine message should allocate a certain period in a day only to study. The person who is unaware of the knowledge and culture of his day has nothing much to say to the people he is dealing with, or in other words, the person whose level of knowledge and culture is shallow cannot long satisfy the minds of the people he is addressing. Therefore, a guide who is likely to meet people at all levels of knowledge and education should at least have sufficient knowledge and the mastery of the issues he is explaining to satisfy the people he is dealing with. It is my belief that anyone who is backward in his cultural epoch can offer but very little to those who are, or think they are, ahead of him.

I insistently and emphatically repeat that those who regard communicating the message as the purpose of their lives should be equipped with learning and knowledge of God. What an empty person will say is also empty, worse still is when such people try to cover their lack by vehemence, belligerence, angry and futile attitudinizing: in reaction to that, those who are listening will be put off and indeed resent what they otherwise would accept as reasonable.

- V -

All work should be done with devotion, from the heart and with sincerity. Seeking the pleasure of God is what should govern the perspective, and everything should be designed and regulated accordingly. The method to be followed and the strategies to be applied should primarily be evaluated and assessed by the pleasure of God. If we have a strong conviction that God will be pleased with them, we will go ahead, otherwise, we should absolutely renounce them, and in this way we may hope never to offer any occasion for people to be misled.

The Prophet defines, limits, struggle in the way of God as that struggle which is undertaken only to exalt the religion of God.[17] That means that if you are striving on the way in order to spread the name of God, then it is for God. But to claim that, while in reality serving one's carnal self, is doomed to failure: for such a struggle is without sincerity and obtains no reward, and where sincerity is damaged, neither the pleasure of God nor any positive influence on the hearts of others are thinkable.

There lived such people before us that whenever they felt that they had spoken or acted flawlessly, they straightaway went into prostration and asked for forgiveness and sincerity from God. For instance, when 'Umar ibn 'Abd al-'Aziz saw how well he had written a state letter, and himself liked its eloquence, he feared lest pride and conceit should enter his heart, and immediately tore up the letter and wrote a new one. Islam was presented in such an atmosphere of sincerity and consciousness then. To speak of God and to spread His message in such a style that the carnal self gained no advantage or comfort from it was almost considered a principle. They assumed that since their own carnal self did not like and get a share from such acts, that there was the pleasure of God in them, and later they turned this into a principle. In sum, sincerity and action from the heart must be the whole essence of what is taught or explained; and if we would avoid reproach and having our efforts thrown back in our faces in the Hereafter, we must stick to sincerity firmly.

We see in many hadiths that the Prophet emphasized the significance of sincerity and indicated it as the ultimate objective or horizon.[18]

In narrating about the Prophets, the Qur'an pointed out their sincerity, and presented it as an integral part of prophethood. The Qur'an concisely tells us in the word *"mukhlas"* (Maryam 19:51) that the Prophet Moses' acts and work were done only to gain the pleasure of God, and in this way it gives people a lesson in sincerity. The Prophet Abraham, as one whose understanding and consciousness of sincerity was of the highest order, did not fall into doubt and despair even when all events and conditions proved against him, and he even refused the intercession of the angels, taking refuge in only God, Who is All-Aware, All-Knowing, All-Seeing, and said, "God is enough for me."[19] What was more important for him was the pleasure of God, and he did not put this idea into a secondary place even when threatened with execution. For this reason he was called *Khalil* (friend) of God[20]; and such a friendship obviously requires the deepest devotion and sincerity.

One day when the Prophet was addressed as "O Friend of God," he immediately reacted with: "No. That is Abraham."[21] Also, one day when he was addressed as *"Sayyiduna,"* (our master) he immediately reacted with: *"Sayyiduna* is Abraham."[22] Thus it is that only a jeweler appreciates the true value of a jewel. That is why, sincerity and action from heart, the attributes of the Prophets, should be inseparable and integral parts of those who take on the duty of the Prophets. The Qur'an presents us every Prophet as one who had achieved sincerity or to whom God commanded it.[23] So, I believe that it would be better to study the Qur'an from this aspect too.

- VI -

Whatever the level the guide has attained, his heart should be equipped with religious sciences and his mind with civil and positive sciences. By employing his skills and talents at a level high above worldly trivialities, a level attained as a result of the union of both kinds of knowledge, he should become more profound in inward self-supervision, and then, within the potentialities granted to him, he should improve in understanding of the Names of God. All of which is, of course, related to the point we made above—the acquisition of sincerity and action from the heart in all their dimensions.

Those who take on the duty of guidance should never indulge in the vulgar ways of getting others to accept them, of having the conceit that they influence people, or of boasting of increase in the number of their followers. Instead, they should make a self-criticism of their actions to see if they conform to the pleasure of God. Self-criticism, self-inspection, and self-supervision are essential with regard to spiritual guidance.

What is the reason for what you are doing? That is what needs to be checked and supervised. If there is anything related to our *nafs* (selfhood, carnal self), we must know to stop there and then. For instance, you are reading and telling something in a gathering, a very good thing in itself, but as you become attentive you realize that what you are captivated by is not the content and meaning of what you are reading but the fact that you are doing so and how well you are doing it. So, there and then, you must stop, or at least pass the book to someone else to carry on. Say, you are preaching from a pulpit, and by the grace of God, you are blessed with such an "expansiveness" that you have only to part your lips and the words flow from your mouth as if of their own accord. There and then you should pay attention to Him Who makes you speak so, and realizing the Giver of such a blessing you should acknowledge your smallness, your servanthood to Him and His Lordship. Otherwise, if your *nafs* is trying to get some share in His Grace, and you are captivated by that, you must know to stop speaking immediately and get down from the pulpit. For, there is *fitna* (severe trial) in speaking well, and one should seek refuge in God from such an end. There have been such orators in the world who led great masses of people behind them, but (except the few who were sincere among them) many of their followers are still giving their accounts bitterly, resentfully, to God of how they were persuaded. Say, we are regularly reading and reciting from the Qur'an as our act of secluded worship, and, while reading, we become aware of also trying to melodize and sweeten our voice. Though it is the Qur'an, even such acts of worship are vulnerable to other aims than the pleasure of God, so doubts arise in us and give us pause. Then we should say, "O God, I have begun to read for You, and now I'm stopping, also for You," and stop reading. Thus, by this inner self-supervision, we learn to regulate ourselves in respect of what is coming up from the depths of our hearts. When it is time, one should know how to deny the carnal self and how to strive against the carnal self. Even in this struggle, one should look for the pleasure of God and act in the ways which will lead to His pleasure.

Such a mood may sometimes manifest in manners that will appear to some people as abnormal, such as, shaking the head, being doubled up in pain, or going into prostration and crying, groaning, there. However, sincerity will, gradually over time, will become natural, and then one can do, act, take or give up everything for God with ease of heart. May God grant us sincerity and purity of heart according to our needs, but not our deserts.

- VII -

If our work causes some adverse reactions in some particular conscience, we should, saying "God's good pleasure (with us) is above all," wholeheartedly and cheerfully give way to another to do the work. Some individuals may react to us for some particular personal reasons, and whatever we say may bring about an adverse reaction. If we remained insisting, our efforts would only serve to make the other refuse, rather than accept. Thus, while that other person has suffered a loss in not accepting the truth, we will suffer a greater loss for we prevented its acceptance. The solution is simple. It is someone else, not we, who will speak to that person. It may be that he accepts the truth from another and so, for being a means to it, however indirect, we will earn the reward for it—as much as the one who worked after us. A subtle matter here is to observe that there is a difference between merely willing that another do the work, and accepting cheerfully that it be so, liking it to be so. We should endeavor to be of the latter, for that is sure to displease the carnal self, and that takes courage and is an instance of genuine altruism and generosity in the cause.

The offer of a Companion who expressed his desire for a position of authority was not welcomed by the Prophet.[24] Similarly, a desire to be the person who speaks at a gathering is not welcomed either. The Prophet always gave such duties to those who were competent, qualified, appropriate and deserving. For this reason, people should come together, choose the person, prepare the conditions for him to speak, and should never be troubled by being among the listeners.

- VIII -

When we encounter issues or questions we have no knowledge of, we should readily and comfortably say "I don't know." Again, our best example and guide is the Prophet. With malicious intent, some Jews came and asked the Prophet about the essence of the spirit, looking to raise doubts and misgivings about his

Prophethood. As the Revelation had not yet come on this matter, the Prophet gave no answer and kept silent; but, later on, the matter was revealed: *Say: The spirit is my Lord's command and you have not been given except a little knowledge* (Isra 17:85). The Prophet's keeping silent in the first place and answering later on, after the verse was revealed, became more influential, and when the Jews got the anticipated answer they were convinced and silenced. So, even the Prophet of God did not say "I know" to every question. What a great lesson to us all!

When the Archangel Gabriel, disguised as a traveler and inquirer, came to the Prophet and asked the time of the Day of Resurrection, the Prophet answered, "the one who is asked does not know more than the one who asks."[25] There cannot be a better example to teach us that we do not have to answer every question put to us.

On one occasion, when Imam Abu Yusuf was asked one hundred questions, he responded to sixty out of the hundred with "I don't know." And the people reacted that they were paying for the position of the Imam, and yet here was the Imam saying "I don't know." Imam Abu Yusuf explained: "You are paying me for the things I know, and if you had paid for what I don't know, the whole world would not have sufficed." Imam Abu Yusuf at that time held the position of Chief *Qadi*. On a similar occasion, Imam Malik answered only three questions out of thirty put to him.

These and similar examples show that even the giants of learning held in the highest honor and esteem for their knowledge, did not answer everything they were asked. What is more, they said, "I don't know." So, we should easily be able to acknowledge that we do not know; but we need not to leave it at that; we must follow up the matter, and seek learning where we are ignorant. It is also possible that there may be a knowledgeable person whom we know and trust, to whom we can take the questioner or the question. In this way, we learn ourselves and prepare opportunities for others to learn also.

- IX -

The people of guidance should be generous, open-handed and benevolent. They should be ready, willing and decisive to spend everything they have in His cause while going on the path of serving God. To win the hearts of people they should make their generosity a means, a vehicle. Whenever generosity is mentioned, Khadija, the wife of the Prophet, comes to my mind. She was born before him and passed away before the Prophet. When she met the future Prophet, she was a noble and prosperous businesswoman, organizing trade caravans to other countries whereas he did not have anything in terms of worldly wealth. However, this woman of great insight perceived the great potential in the future Prophet and proposed to him. She had a nature suited to becoming the wife of the Prophet. When Prophethood was given to him, she was the first to acknowledge him, without any doubt, and put the whole of her wealth at his disposal, in the way of God. Nothing was left from this wealth during the boycott imposed upon the Muslims by Quraysh in Makka. At times the Prophet could not find anything to eat and was all but fainting with weakness because there had been nothing at home for days. During that time, *umm al-mu'minin* (mother of believers) Khadija became ill and as there were no means to procure treatment, she passed away. In generosity, the ultimate is to give oneself, to be consumed.

Abu Bakr was one of the richest tradesmen in Makka, but as one of the good examples of generosity, he used and spent all his wealth in the way of God, and nothing was left to him and his family. He used to distract his aged father by putting pebbles into the money bag, while spending the pieces of gold in the way of Islam. For this reason, even when he was elected the Caliph, he was one of the poor and earned his living by milking other people's sheep.[26]

'Umar and his family subsisted on a few dates, as did the poorest in Madina. That suggests that he too used up everything he had in the way of God.[27]

The Companions of the Prophet competed with each other in acts of generosity and altruism on behalf of Islam. Their sincere generosity won hearts and minds to Islam, and the number of entrants to the faith grew with the gathering force of an avalanche. In this as in all matters, the Companions took their cue from the Prophet. One day, one of those on the brink of entering the faith who had yet to do so, went to his tribe and said: "O my tribe! Go and surrender to that person, for he is the Prophet of God. If he had not been a Prophet, he would not have been so generous, and feared for his sustenance. This person gives immediately whoever wants whatever."[28]

Every spiritual teacher young or old, should try to enter and conquer the hearts of people in this way. If one gains the heart of a person by spending all he has, he will be considered to have gained a lot and lost nothing. For the generous will open the gates of Paradise.[29] So, one should open the ways that lead to such gates in this world so that there are many to accompany one to Paradise in the other world. Those whom you treated with generosity in this world will be in a state such that if one day they happen to face a choice between human-improvised way of life and Qur'an-enjoined ways, they will choose the Qur'an and the Prophet and so come to submit, to surrender, themselves, wholly to God.

Those who are first to enter the Paradise will not be scholars or preachers, lecturers or teachers, rather those—whoever they are, whether big businessmen or small, or ordinary workers, disposing large incomes or small—who spent their wealth and lives on the path to spread the Truth; generous, open-handed, benevolent and altruistic Muslims, profoundly attached and devoted to God alone. For it is they who were able to distinguish rightly and accordingly it will be said of them: they gave to their Lord what is transitory and perishable and received what is permanent and everlasting.

- X -

Today we witness and experience an awakening of consciousness in all walks of life such as we have not experienced for almost twenty years. In the past it was really difficult to find so many believers in the field of higher education as there are today. This is a sheer blessing of God. However, now, not individuals but the masses stand as the owners, protectors or patrons of services to Islam. We experience a time when even some of the most obstinate people have come to soften their attitudes to Islamic matters and even begun to consider them as feasible. Therefore, at such a time, it is incumbent upon us to develop, employ and evaluate new methods and approaches, provided that we do not depart from the essence and spirit of the truth. Otherwise, it is likely, indeed certain, that we will, as others have, fail to realize the conditions of the time and so lose relevance and effectiveness. We take refuge in God from falling into such a state. We must, as we need to do, adapt to the new ways and developments that the present age presents to us. It should be remembered that the slower we are to adapt, the slower we shall be in reaching the target.

We may conclude with a point that is general and valid for all, that those who take on spiritual guidance should know and realize the conditions and requirements of their epoch, and base their ways of working on these fundamentals. While others are returning into space and shuttling between far new horizons, it is obvious that we will get nowhere by taking people to unsophisticated ways, dark places or underground, in order to teach them something.

- XI -

Understanding group psychology, using appropriate ways to facilitate the joining and progressing of new people is also important. With some people there are things you speak of but cannot make understood for years. Make such people aware of the development and progress of particular services and institutions, get them to see and meet the others who are working sincerely, whole-heartedly and with great zeal, let them feel the value and atmosphere of cooperation, solidarity and mutual help in collective work. Such direct witnessing may prove more influential than mere telling. However, the Islamic services and institutions should be presented without discrimination and prejudice, without any sense of exclusivity or belonging to a narrow grouping or party. Such visits and demonstrations can influence and reinforce the people's power of determination in such a way that they may jump the interval of years on one occasion, and be ready to stand on the same line as yourself, shoulder to shoulder. This is true of both individuals and groups.

Thank God that such institutions are now great in numbers, both to hearten the believers and to dishearten the enemies of Islam.

3.4.

How should we deal with mockery or ridicule, especially of the young trying to practice their religion by their peers?

Forthwith he [Noah] starts constructing the Ark: Every time that the Chiefs of his people passed by him they threw ridicule on him. He said: "If you ridicule us now, we (in our turn) can look down on you with ridicule likewise! But soon will you know who it is on whom will descend a chastisement that will cover them with shame—on whom will be unloosed a chastisement lasting." (Hud 11:38-9)

"Our Lord! bring us out of this: if ever we return (to evil), then shall we be wrongdoers indeed!" He will say: "Be you driven into it (with ignominy)! And speak you not to Me! A part of My servants there was, who used to pray, "Our Lord! we believe; then do You forgive us, and have mercy upon us: for You are the Best of those who show mercy!" But you treated them with ridicule, so much so that (ridicule of) them made you forget My message while you were laughing at them! I have rewarded them this day for their patience and constancy. They are indeed the ones that have achieved bliss . . ." (Mu'minun 23:107-11)

Those in sin used to laugh at those who believed, and whenever they passed by them, used to wink at each other (in mockery); and when they returned to their own people, they would return jesting. (Mutaffifin 83:29-31)

It is clear from the verses above that the Qur'an regards derision and ridicule of the believers as a habit, a regular custom, characteristic of unbelievers. A Muslim may neither initiate nor return derision and ridicule of the beliefs of others: that is explicitly commanded in the Qur'an, where the reason given is that the Muslim must not provoke unbelievers into one of the greatest sins, namely blasphemy, even if the unbelievers do not recognize it as such.

Those who ridicule the believers will clearly see what they did; they will have a clear answer for it in the Hereafter, and will there curse and denounce themselves. In the brief life of this world, retaliation in kind exacerbates the harm and there is no point in that. As believers, we are enjoined not to retaliate in such situations, and we are most content with this injunction to restraint.

Believing in God and expressing surrender and servanthood to Him is the highest glory and honor for us in this world and the next. If it were permissible, we would take pride in it and boast of it.

The mockers mock our prayer, but it is our means of ascension, that makes us closer to our Creator. They mock our *wudu'* (ablution); it will make us known to our Prophet beside the pool of *kawthar* (heavenly river) through the radiance it brings to our faces. They mock our manner of dress; it is what the Prophet commended as the way that increases our reward manifold and us in dignity. None of these are worthy of ridicule; rather, they are ways that will be acknowledged and prized for their supreme otherworldly value and reward in the Hereafter.

What is worthy of criticism is the manner of one who spurns the Creator like, or worse than, an ignorant animal. Likewise deserving of criticism are the manners of drunks, dipsomaniacs who shame and disgrace themselves and their society: of usurers, black-marketeers, monopolists, and profiteers, who defraud and disgrace the commercial life of the society; of those who profit from the weaknesses of others by systematically encouraging and exaggerating those weaknesses, drug-pushers, the dealers in pornography and the so-called sex "industry."

Yet those who take up or support shameful practices aspire to spread them, and resent those who keep themselves aloof, safe, from their poison. Out of that resentment, their ridicule is born, and especially directed at the young. To the young Muslims so targeted, we say: find strength, assurance and solace in this description of your character:

> Those who witness no falsehood and if they pass by futility, they pass by it with honorable (avoidance). (Furqan 25:72)

So when young religious Muslims, who are honored by the Qur'an, find themselves in such a situation, they must withdraw from it in an honorable, dignified way. If they pass by those putting on impertinent and doubtful attitudes, let them pass noble-heartedly, kindly and smilingly, and thus demonstrate the strength and contentment, the sheer sanity and ease, of being a Muslim. Those who mock display their own smallness of spirit. Let the young Muslims answer their smallness with largesse: behave to them with dignified seriousness, retain your natural courtesy of manner and speech, present the strength of Islam with all its grace and sweetness. Indeed, offer in your heart that even those mockers may find guidance to the Right Path. For that is most becoming to a Muslim, and will be a proof for yourselves of being on the Muhammadi way.

Each of us shall be resurrected with what we did. Those who laugh at Muslims today will be exposed to laughter and ridicule; those who are ridiculed today will be honored and glorified with the kindness and favor of God tomorrow, and they will pass over the bridge of *Sirat* (the very narrow bridge which leads to Heaven) like lightning, and reach the Garden of Paradise.

May God make firm the feet of those young Muslims subjected to the assaults of ridicule and scorn in the way of Islam; may they never be shaken nor made fearful, nor caused to step back from that way. May God grant them the strength and grace to see the great journey to its end. Amin.

3.5.

As God already gives His blessings and peace to Prophet Muhammad, what is the wisdom in our invoking God's blessings and peace upon him? Does he need our invocations?

P rophet Muhammad is like the core of all the good deeds, prosperity and divine blessing. He is the unfailing, unerring guide, the exemplar to be taken as a model by all, and the one who leads to the Right Path, who establishes the best methods to serve God and humankind and thus ushers a new era to enable human beings to live humanely.

He is the means, appointed by God, to take people out of darkness to the light. Accordingly, he will be given the equal of the reward earned by the good deeds of his community. In accordance with the principle "one who causes is like the doer,"[30] the same amount of reward for the good and righteous deeds done by his people will go on being written in his book of reward till the Day of Judgment.

To the Prophet belongs the *Maqam al-Mahmud*, the praised position or rank assigned to him as intercessor in the Day of Judgment. His book of reward will not be closed from the time of his death. Rather, abundance of good works and pious deeds will be added to it, his rank will increase ever higher, the scope of his intercession will expand further,[31] and thus, as God wills, he will have a right to intercede for greater numbers, masses, of the people of his community. For this reason, we will look at this question from two different angles:

First, by uttering the formula calling God's benediction on the Prophet, we renew our oath to the Prophet and the desire to belong among his community. That is, we say: "We remembered and thought of you as our Prophet and prayed God to increase your worth and degree, and we join and relate ourselves to you." Since our prayer is made with the intention that God will increase the degree of esteem of the owner of the *Maqam al-Mahmud*, his sphere of intercession will expand and thus many more people will be able to benefit from his intercession on the Day of Judgment.

Secondly, one's prayer to God that the Prophet's rank be increased is a means to be taken under the protection of the Prophet and thus one's hope of intercession is enlarged. That is why it is we, rather than the Prophet, who are in need of invoking God's blessings and peace upon him. By doing so we acknowledge the Prophet as the Prophet, his greatness and authority, and, at the same time we acknowledge our smallness, our nothingness, our need for belonging to his community. Just as a person can regard the state of which he is a subject or citizen as potent to assist him in case of need or danger, so do we stand in need, on account of our incompetence, poverty, and the anxiety of a terrible Day of Reckoning—even now, in advance, we can feel the oncoming, shock of that Day— of the refuge and safety of the Prophet, and we seek that refuge through our invocations, inform him of our present state and give him a petition to be remembered.

May God honor us with the intercession of His Prophet, the one who has by God's leave, the widest right of intercession on the Day of Reckoning.

Reflect, too, on the good news that God allows to every Prophet something that he may pass on to his people. When the other Prophets were granted the right to ask something for their peoples, they all asked for something in this world. But our Prophet said: "I left what I would give to my people to the Hereafter, and that is my intercession."[32]

CHAPTER 4

Scientific Issues

4.1.

Is it right when people link HIV to "the Beast of the Earth" (Dabbat al-ard), one of the signs of the Last Day?

T he question touches on two matters. One has to do with what AIDS is; the other has to do with how Muslims as Muslims make sense of it and of similar phenomena. Let us take the first matter first.

What is AIDS?

AIDS or Acquired Immune Deficiency Syndrome is a viral infection which destroys the body's defenses against disease. Because its effects are dramatic and nearly always fatal, it has been called the plague of modern times. It also spreads very quickly—the number of people infected is reckoned to be doubling every ten months. Moreover, there is, as yet, no reported cure.

AIDS was first diagnosed in 1981. Once initial investigations into it—how the infection is transmitted, how it develops and progresses, and the difficulty of containing, let alone curing, it—became widely known, the popular reaction was panic.

No such infection had been reported before the eighties. How did it originate? Among other conspiracy theories, one was that the virus had "escaped" from improperly controlled experiments in the United States for biological or chemical warfare purposes. There is no proof for this allegation. Nor is there any proof for the other popular theory that the disease originated among a particular species of monkey in Africa, "jumped" into a human being, and was then carried, through sexual contact, to an American visiting Africa who then took it back with him to the United States whence it spread further. The reality is that nobody knows how HIV originated.

There is certain knowledge, however, of how the disease is transmitted. It is transmitted by direct exchange of bodily fluids; in the United States and Canada HIV is most commonly transmitted during sex between homosexual men and by sharing needles while using illicit drugs. Transfusion of infected blood can also cause the disease, and it can be passed on by infected pregnant women to their babies.

It is also known with certainty that some people may be HIV carriers, able to transmit the disease to others without suffering the effects of it themselves. This adds further to the mystery and terror surrounding HIV.

HIV may be epidemic in some parts of the world but, all praise and thanks to God, the least infected peoples are Muslims, whether in Muslim countries or others. The noble values and morality of the Islamic way of life have protected Muslims against such a disaster, even though they have suffered a long and intensive campaign to renounce that way of life. HIV is a visible feature of the impurities that flow under (or along with) so much of the mainstream of the "modern lifestyle"; but, for reasons that need not been gone into here, I think it better to avoid dwelling on the useless, on what is vain or absurd or immoral. To be frank, even talking around an issue like HIV causes me considerable unease and embarrassment. I therefore touch upon the subject only so far as it can be approached in a way that benefits the understanding and well-being of right-minded people.

Now, as to the second matter. How should Muslims as Muslims make sense of HIV?

How to respond to phenomena like HIV

It is, unfortunately, true that some people have put forward the view that HIV is the referent of the Qur'anic phrase *dabbat al-*

ard which means, literally, "beast of the earth," whose appearance will indicate the nearness of the Last Day. We shall look
closely at the content of this view, but there is a general point
here which also needs to be discussed.

To read *dabbat al-ard* as referring to HIV is a particular
example of a more general failure to be sufficiently careful in
relying upon modern referents for terms used in the Qur'an and
hadith. A specific example is the hasty interpretation by some
people—intending no doubt to affirm the "scientific validity" of
hadith—of the Prophet's warning: "Flee from leprosy just as
you would from a lion."[1] These people thought the metaphor of
lion very telling because the microbe associated with leprosy
seemed to look like a lion. Closer microscopic inspection proved
this likeness to be incorrect. Now if any Muslim had believed
that what the Prophet said had anything whatever to do with
the form of the leprosy microbe, would that Muslim's belief not
be vulnerable to the argument that a statement attributed to the
Prophet had been established as false.

To make claims of the sort just illustrated can be harmful.
To do so without knowledge and understanding of the essential
truth of the matter in question is surely wrong. Besides, none of
the findings of scientific research are ever absolute. Neither the
procedures of research, nor the processes of reasoning about the
results of research, are free from error. Indeed, the most widely
accepted position among scientists themselves is that the best to
be hoped for from science is the gradual elimination, one by
one, of past *and* present errors. Extreme positivist or rationalist
doctrines are now generally rejected. It seems most improper,
therefore, to seek to understand or explain the Qur'an or hadith
on the basis of what is, *at best*, uncertain and hypothetical, and
quite possibly false. The great volume of articles and books produced in this vein in recent times will be open to ridicule in the
future. To be sure, there is a reward for sincerity and good intention; but what if sincerity and good intention result in weakening faith and practice instead of strengthening them? What if

they lead to Muslims being embarrassed and mocked on account of the naiveté of the arguments put forward on behalf of Islam? It is our view that people who have approached the subject of HIV in this way have erred.

It is surely wiser, worthier in intention and result, to tackle such subjects from a broad, traditionally Islamic perspective. Arguments that do so, however "old" remain fresh, light and appealing. The scope and manner of their explanations maintain a link with the general truths of Islam. Precisely for that reason, they are able to embrace the realities specific to particular circumstances and are therefore always relevant and enlightening. By contrast, arguments that bow to the agenda of modern circumstances are (when they are not wrong to start with) soon out of date.

The traditional teaching begins from the belief that God *is*, and Muhammad is His Messenger. It proceeds to explain how particular events or entities in the universe, from the smallest to the largest, affirm that belief. That is wholly different from the approach that begins with the assertion of the so-called truths of science, and then hopes, on the basis of such weak, insecure foundations, to build understanding and knowledge of the Creator and the teaching of His Messenger.

I do not doubt that the Muslims who try to reconcile current knowledge and current events with the Qur'an and hadith are well-intentioned. In doing this, they mean to affirm the statements of the Qur'an and hadith. As against certain attitudes provoked by over-confidence in the natural sciences, in positivism and rationalism, they aim to demonstrate that Qur'an and hadith do not contradict but concur with the results of experimentally verified scientific inquiry. They hope to communicate something about Islam to those scholars, thinkers and their students, whose world-view is too narrowly circumscribed by the norms and procedures of scientific investigation. For the reasons explained above, their efforts are sure to receive some criticism in the future. However, to say that their approach is *totally* or *only* harmful would be an ill-considered and hasty judgment. The wisdom of Qur'an and hadith do not need any external support—their authority, soundness, and rightness appeal directly and naturally to human intuition and conscience. That said, we should not over-criticize sincere efforts to present *additional*, external evidence that tries to get rid of the dust that prevents our poor minds from grasping the correspondences or compatibilities between the absolute truths of Islam and the insecure "truths" of science; but what we must, and do, reject is that the truth of Qur'an and hadith should be made to depend upon verification and confirmation by scientific data which are, as explained above, incomplete, disconnected from the meaning and purpose of life as a whole, and vulnerable to change as the borders of human ignorance change.

Let me now turn to the matter of HIV in relation to *dabbat al-ard*.

Dabbat al-ard

The phrase occurs both in the Qur'an and hadith. *Dabba* connotes any entity that creeps, crawls or moves upon the earth on its legs. God describes in the Qur'an all species of animate (moving) creatures of the earth as *dabba*:

> God has created every being (creature) from water: of them there are some that creep on their bellies; some that walk on two legs; and some that walk on four. God creates what He wills. For God has power over all things. (Nur 24:45)

From its use in its context, we see that *dabba* could refer to any of the creatures known to humankind, from micro-organisms to dinosaurs. Yet, there are some that are not known to us, and still others that God will create in the future, as He wills. The HIV virus which leads to AIDS may be among those micro-organisms which have recently become known.

The term is used again, in other Qur'anic verses, when God affirms that He provides sustenance for each of the creatures of the earth. For example:

> There is no moving creature on earth but its sustenance depends on God . . . . (Hud 11:6)

> How many are the creatures that carry not their own sustenance. It is God who feeds both them and you . . . (Ankabut 29:60)

But the *dabba* mentioned in the question occurs in this verse in the chapter *Naml*:

> And when the word is fulfilled against them (the unjust), We shall produce from the earth a *dabba* (beast) to face them. It will speak to them, because humankind did not believe with assurance in our signs. (Naml 27:82)

The "when" to which the verse alludes is that time when the task for which all creatures were created, namely to display the Names and Attributes of God, is concluded, and the earth is no longer needed to serve as an arena of exhibition. Such an exhibition was held because God wills Himself to be known and affirmed. When God is not known and humanity turns away from His signs and rejects the Truth, when the believers, gradually decreasing in number, are finally no more, and the corrupted world is no longer needed, God will decree both human beings and the world to be destroyed. In order to fulfill this decree, God will produce a *dabba*, which speaks, from the earth. Whether it speaks by voice or gesture or by some other means, it will tell that there will no longer be sincere believers in the signs of God from then on. That is, the appearance of *dabba* will signify that the quality of belief and of believers will no longer improve, but rather decay and weaken and eventually become extinct. Moreover, the fact that the verses alluding to Resurrection come just after the verse just quoted indicates that *dabbat al-ard* is among the most important and last of the signs of the end of the world.

Dabbat al-ard is one, probably the last, of the ten signs of the Last Day.[2] Study of the verse in its context, makes it clear that all Islamic life, movements and values, will come to an end, new believers will not succeed those before them, and those who believe in God will lack conviction and certainty (*yaqin*). One explanation is that science and philosophy will have progressed so far, such enthralling technological inventions and discoveries will have been made—human beings, keen on "creating" something, will have attempted to manufacture human beings; they will have produced robots and tried to deliver the administration of affairs to them—that the world will be filled with individuals claiming (and believing) that "I created this or that." And people who make such a claim can never attain certainty (*yaqin*) in their faith and knowledge of God. That is a part of what could be inferred from the full context of the verse.

Dabbat al-ard occurs in the hadiths of the Prophet with the same general meaning as in the Qur'an. The hadiths point out the things *dabba* will do, such as: "*Dabba* will emerge, travel all over the earth and be seen everywhere . . ."

Now as to whether *dabbat al-ard* has anything to do with HIV:

Can HIV be associated in any way with dabbat al-ard?

Firstly, while it may be correct to say that HIV is one aspect or one part of the whole reality of *dabbat al-ard*, it is not correct to say that it *is dabbat al-ard*. For, if HIV is made the only referent of the phrase, the relevance of the verse is thereby restricted and would not survive the problem of HIV. Many diseases have visited humankind in the past, devastated many lives, and later been cured or forgotten. Abu Dawud narrates a hadith from Umm Salama: "God did not create an illness but He provided its cure."[3] In other hadiths, we learn that only death and growing old are incurable.[4] That means that there must be a cure for AIDS, as it were, waiting to be discovered.

Secondly: while there are indeed many cases of AIDS in some countries, the epidemic is nowhere near of the dimensions reached by (for example) tuberculosis in the past; nor, in the present, does it affect as many people as does cancer. These illnesses might also be referred to as *dabbat al-ard*. In fact, in view of the numbers of their victims, it might be more appropriate to do so. However, we should qualify any such statement by adding explicitly that tuberculosis or cancer, likewise, could only be *aspects* of the whole reality of *dabbat al-ard*. Tuberculosis and the plague were defeated by the medication and treatment granted by God to humankind, and (almost) erased from the book of *dabbat al-ard*. Some cancers in early stages of growth can now be successfully treated. May the treatment of HIV also be soon found. The plague used to be a nightmare for people in the past. In Amwas, it killed 30,000 people from among the Companions.[5] We rarely hear of such large death-tolls now, except for a very few incidents in remote parts of the world. That plague, because it caused such widespread and fatal epidemics, might well have been called *dabbat al-ard*. But it was not. Similarly, at the present time, cancer is a great killer all over the world. But, by God, improved treatments and a cure will be found. Now, in terms of the death-toll arising from it, cancer is a likelier candidate for the description of *dabbat al-ard* than HIV. But when cures are found for either or both, do not those who insist upon a narrow interpretation of either as *dabbat al-ard*, risk leading people toward a weakening of their trust in the Qur'an and hadith?

The phenomenon of HIV may well be one aspect of the whole reality of *dabbat al-ard* or carry out one part of the work that *dabbat al-ard* is to do in the future. Similarly, cancer may be the same sort of thing and undertake a small part of the work of *dabbat al-ard*. On the other hand, *dabbat al-ard* itself, which is a great sign and means of declaring to human beings that true faith is wearing away, something that, as we indicated earlier, may follow from the abuse of science and technology, is a unique entity, very different from its constituent aspects. It will be a phenomenon far removed from the familiar and, on account of its sheer oddity, its being alien (*gharaba*), difficult to grasp.

As we noted above, the emergence of *dabbat al-ard* will mark the end of all Islamic values. However, as stated in the eighth verse of the chapter Saf in the Qur'an: *God will most certainly complete His Light* (His favor of Islam). Now, if *dabbat al-ard* were indeed to appear on the earth, it would be a fatal blow to our hopes, because its appearance signals the end of certain belief (*yaqin*) and knowledge of God. There will be an end of it and decline from then on. But, as we know that there will be an Islamic revival and awakening, that once again Islam will gain its due position in the balance of the world, and that the Muslims world-wide will seek and find the guidance of their Prophet Muhammad let us have done with talking about *dabbat al-ard*! We are not expecting it now. It will appear very near the Judgment Day, which is a time of terror for unbelievers. To hold a contrary view is in opposition to belief and a blow to our hopes.

If speculation may be permitted on such a matter, there are many entities, real or potential, which could be candidates for the role of *dabbat al-ard*. Mechanized imitations of human beings or advanced robots—something that, for the present, mainly preoccupies science fiction writers—to which people have consigned rule over their affairs are a possibility. Now the Qur'an indicates that there are entities yet to come into existence whose nature is known only to God and is not knowable by human beings. That is, these entities will be wholly alien to how human beings think or feel: lacking any notion of compassion, the robots—should they turn hostile—will not heed human excuses, pleas, tears—nothing will move them.

Such a possibility gives considerable cause for alarm, even to the very scholars and scientists managing and developing the technology to produce such machines—so much so, that they envisage the possibility that after these advanced robots have been programmed and launched into space, they may defy their instructions (malfunction) and start to fight and devastate everything. If such machines can really exist, they might well be considered a serious candidate to be *dabbat al-ard*.

However, these are no more than speculative musings. We too should be cautious and prudent. Self-operated, self-maintained and motivated advanced machines, or concocted viruses, inexplicable epidemics, minuscule, abhorrent creatures yet to appear, unknown factors in diseases resulting from use of so-called weapons of mass destruction—any of these might represent *dabbat al-ard*, which speaks the death of, first, the human spirit and, then, of the body.

It seems to me that approaching the subject of *dabbat al-ard* in this way may, firstly, preserve respect for the relevant hadiths and verses of the Qur'an, and secondly, not improperly restrict their meaning.

To summarize: I certainly hold that those who relate phenomena like HIV to Islamic sources without sufficient reflection and caution are nevertheless quite sincere in their intentions. But sincerity is only one aspect of dealing responsibly with such multifaceted questions; interpreting them in the way they do is wrong and misleading. Personal sincerity is one thing; being respectful and loyal to the essential truths of hadith and Qur'an is quite another.

What do you say about sperm banks and artificial insemination?

Sperm banks are established to facilitate artificial insemination. It has been used for plants and animals for a long time to produce higher quality breeds and to improve and preserve the species. However, its widespread use for humans is recent.

The seed in the plant kingdom and the sperm in the animal kingdom are the indexes and data boxes of the new beings. The seed germinates in the soil and the sperm in the womb. They are the kernels from which the attributes and characteristics of the new being develop. They are the elements through which the procreation and survival of the species are maintained.

While in the plant and animal kingdom artificial insemination has some significance in terms of the preservation and improvement of the species, its usage in humans is fixed by certain legal principles. In addition, it also needs to be dealt with in terms of the natural laws governing the universe (*shari'at al-fitra*).

We accept without argument artificial insemination for plants and animals. However, for human beings, because of inheritance, marriage, and family relationships, it represents a very different situation. For those reasons, the manner of fertilization and procreation has been bound by restrictions since the first human in the world, and it has come to our day as it was, except for a few periods of history during which it was abused.

This may have been because of humankind's unlimited carnal desire or because of some natural disposition. We strongly hold that the first union of man and woman was bound by divine restrictions. Since the beginning of legislation, the protection of lineage has been one of the five basic principles (*usul al-khamsa*). This basic principle tells us that the sperm and the womb must be restricted and tied to each other by a contract. In other words, the sperm and womb should be tied and the reality of male and female, which seem to be separate, become symbolically united. Through this union, the third aspect of the family, i.e. the child, acquires its legitimate affinity to the family union. The religion sees this union as marriage. It is the most firm foundation on which the family can be established.

Any union of sperm and womb without marriage is considered fornication. It leads to the destruction of the family trio, widespread immorality, women being debased to the level of common property, and illegitimacy. For this reason, the Divine religions all place special emphasis on marriage. They consider it a necessary condition of being a human. On the other hand, adultery and fornication are considered to be transgression and delirium caused by uncontrolled, base human nature.

If fertilization is caused by a sperm of unknown origin, can it be legitimate? In fact, there is no difference between a child born through this manner and one born of an illicit relationship. Since there is no contract in either of these cases, lineage is broken and the family tree is felled. From this arise several legal issues which cannot be overcome: e.g. inheritance, marriage and family relationships. For this reason, artificial insemination is not a subject which can be dealt with lightly. Apart from this, in terms of a psycho-sociological approach or of family psychology this issue presents many risks. A father who knows that the child was not born from his own sperm cannot erase the feeling of strangeness toward the innocent child who he himself is trying to attentively bring up. He will always approach him with a degree of fearful uncertainty. In this way, it also affects the mother and her way of looking at both the child and the father and the relationship between them. The child will carry a double burden. He may perceive the paternal closeness of his father as a mere loan. He will feel he is wearing the borrowed shirt of sonhood. I say "perceived" because it will be heard from somewhere that he is not the real son or he may gather this from the looks and attitude of his supposed father.

They may ask "if the sperm is taken from the woman's husband, is artificial insemination then permitted?" To say yes to such a question without careful consideration may be taken as a religious-legal responsum (*fatwa*). This is because the nature of the question seems to elicit a positive answer, but the bad intention behind it and the demagogy implied in it leads us to be cautious. Why do they choose such an unnatural way, while there is a natural and innate way? Would it not be appropriate to submit to Divine wisdom and act according to the rules of physical creation? To comply with the natural way is essential. For this reason, artificial insemination is completely unnatural and institutions serving it might be considered tacitly the institutions of fornication.

They may raise another question. They may say: "What you said may be true when the father is able to fertilize and the mother is able to be fertilized. In this case one certainly takes the natural way. However, what about when the father is not able to do so?" Then I will ask the question: "Whose sperm is used in fertilization?" If the father is weak, impotent and the sperm does not function as it is supposed to then it is obvious that the sperm taken from the father will definitely not fertilize the egg. One will then take foreign sperm and this will be considered indirect fornication. If the situation is because the mother has a blockage or inadequacy or sickness of the womb, the specialist should intervene. If such a legal medical intervention makes the womb "a place of rest firmly fixed" (Mu'minun 23:13), then it becomes incumbent to follow the natural way. If the womb is not able to function as it is supposed to, artificial insemination is meaningless. Taking this subject lightly and saying "taking the sperm from the husband is permitted," although technically true, is a defective judgment because it is open to abuse. Indeed, I do fear that those who raise such issues do so in order to get a judgment of a sort to open the doors to abuse. Sperm banks are already in existence and their doors are wide open to anyone whether they consider artificial insemination legitimate in Islam or not.

In terms of the laws of nature (*shari'at al-fitriya*), artificial insemination has many objections. However, discussing them opens up a complicated debate and so I will not enter into it. It is not my field. I should leave it to the specialists, scientists and doctors; that is the soundest approach.

There is no doubt that such a way is contrary to nature. Every being is urged to maintain the survival of the species through sexual reproduction. They are given a small reward in the form of temporary pleasure to serve this end. The Owner of all beings who imbued such a disposition into beings does not want it to be changed. Therefore, no one has any right to seek to abolish this natural phenomenon. Any attempt to do so is an attempt to change creation and nature, which must be rejected (*mardud*) as satanic. It is an approach that considers humans at the level of plants and animals and destroys the distinction of humanity. For this reason, each and every person ought to protest against such thinking. However, people of today are crawling at the ABC of natural sciences. It will not be easy to save them from the madness of hastily contrived technologies. Some are no doubt seeking an artificial conflict on this and similar issues between science and the creation of humanity "in the best pattern" (Tin 95:4), and seeking to present science and religion as in opposition to one another.

We hope that such people who are in a sort of delirium soon wake up and see the truth, and that all the obstructions in the way between science and ethics will be overcome.

4.3.

What is the reason for the persistence of Darwinism in the general culture of the masses, though many of Darwin's hypotheses have been challenged and even disproved?

I t would be difficult to find another theory which, like Darwinism, has been battered and defeated so many times, and yet the corpse of it revived artificially again and again. Some scientists still defend it to the hilt; others discredit it altogether, asserting that holding to it is sheer delusion. It seems that, in the academic-scientific world, Darwinism will keep conference agendas busy for some time yet, and thousands more articles and books will be written on it, and the debates persist.

The collapse of communism as an ideology and as a political force has made it more obvious than it was before that "East" and "West" was a geographical, not a cultural divide. It was and is right to think of the experiment in Russia and its former satellite states as a variation within Western culture, not an opposition to it. The strictly Western attitude to religion, derived from Rousseau and Renan, was to see it as a socially necessary myth, a delusion that provided a sort of cultural and social cohesion to collective life but which had no more basis in reality than do dreams. The strictly Eastern (Communist) attitude, founded upon explicit rejection of religion and explicit acceptance of materialism, naturally favored Darwinism (which entails the same rejection) and gave to it more deliberate and institutional support than in the West. But in the broader view, modern Western culture as a whole is closely predicated on the assumptions of Darwinism, and those who, in Muslim countries, wish to promote Western culture, continue, in universities and educational institutions generally, to pass off Darwinism as established scientific truth and, by implication, to represent religion as unscientific and false. Inevitably, some of this poison is effective on pliable young minds: many of them begin to believe (though far fewer continue to believe) that religion is not conformable to human reason, and that, as an explanation of the origin of species, Darwinism is still the best that independent human reason can do.

I will not go into the details of the evolutionary hypothesis, but within the scope of brief question and answer, I will touch upon some of the major points.

According to Darwin, life originated on earth from simple, single-celled organisms giving rise to multi-cellular organisms through a process of gradual change, along with random mutations, over millions of years. According to more developed forms of evolutionary theory, the foundation of all living things is amino acids within water, which later somehow got formed into single-celled organisms, like the amoeba, and these organisms interacting with each other and the immediate environment over uncalculated billions of years, gradually or by sudden jumps evolved into the great variety of complex multi-cellular animals. Then the invertebrates gave rise to aquatic vertebrates, i.e., fish, which evolved into amphibians which gave rise to reptiles; later, some reptiles evolved into birds, while others evolved into mammals culminating in the evolution of humankind.

The hypothesis is typically argued on the basis of a few incomplete pieces of fossils, though, so far, the actual fossil record has failed to endorse that view. To our knowledge, no scientific hypothesis except this one was ever sustained on the basis of so many, and so important "missing links." What the scientists have discovered through observation proves the opposite of the evolutionary theory true: in spite of having many varieties, bacteria have not evolved into anything different and higher though they adapt very quickly; in whatever variety they exist, cockroaches and insects have been living as they are for almost 350 million years. Fruit flies have remained fruit flies for millions of years; arthropoda, sponges, and sea crabs today are exactly as found in fossils from rock formations formed 500 million years ago; snakes, lizards, mice, and many other species, have not evolved into any other different species; nor have horse's hooves or human feet evolved into something different. Man is, as we put it, exactly the same as he was created on the first day.

There are no examples of the transitional organisms that the theory requires, such as, for example, an animal that has evolved its front legs *partly* (but not yet wholly) into wings in readiness for the transition to bird-like flight. And, unsurprisingly, there is not even a theoretical explanation, given that such transitions are supposed to take thousands of generations to complete. How the partly evolved animal could survive in what kind of environment—lacking four "good" legs, and still not equipped with two good legs and a pair of wings.

Many arguments give the erroneous example of the evolution of the horse from a small dog-like mammal with five toes to the large modern horse with one toe or hoof. In fact, the evolutionists have no evidence for that claim. Nowhere in the world have they found a series of fossils to demonstrate such an evolutionary order. It remains entirely hypothetical, suppositional. They talk about an animal which lived in the past and claim that it was the ancestor of the modern horse; but they cannot establish any necessary connection between the modern horse and that animal: the only need for that connection is the need to illustrate the theory, which the illustration is supposed to establish. This is the very opposite of reliable scientific argument and procedure. We shall say that God created such an animal at that age which later on became extinct, and it no longer exists now. Why do we need to connect these two species? Even today horses of different sizes and breeds co-exist in our age.

Scientists found bees and honey from millions of years ago. The bee produced honey and the honeycomb in the same way as it does today, using the same geometrical measures, 100 million years ago. So, for that whole expanse of time neither the bee's brain and physiological structure nor the way it produces honey have changed.

What of the evolution of humankind? It is especially badly argued and ill-founded. Some scientist discovered some bones, or even just the tooth of an ape, and posited (that is, guessed) the rest—the body posture, flesh, skin, hair, features, etc., of the evolved "human."

Piltdown Man is a good example to famous scientific hoaxes related with evolution. The supposed discovery near Piltdown, England, of an ape-like fossil ancestral to modern humans, was reported in 1912. The discovery included fragments of what were later proved to be a modern human cranium and the jawbone of an ape. For many years the Pildown man fossil was a subject of anthropological controversy. In 1953, scientific analyses proved the fossil a forgery.

Evolutionists used to mention the coelacanth, a fish abundant 400 million years ago, as a link between the fish and the land-animals because of its limb-like fins. It was theorized that the coelacanth lurched onto the land in search of food, staying there longer and longer until—about 70 million years ago—it disappeared from the fossil record. To their surprise, local fishermen caught several dozen coelacanths off the coast of Madagascar in 1938. The caught fish were exactly like their ancestors, perfectly adapted to their deep-sea environment and showing no signs of evolution. The coelacanth has been quietly dropped by many text books from the list of evidences of evolution, because it became the symbol of the non-evolution of organisms, rather than of their evolution.

Evolutionists also claim that the organisms evolve through random mutations. While new cells are being formed, if the genetic code, normally identical in all the cells of an organism, is copied differently or mistakenly, mutations occur. Such a change, which is claimed to bear evolutionary fruit gradually over a long period, may be caused by a number of external agents, such as geography and climate, even planetary influences such as changes in the sun's or earth's rotation, or by radiation, chemical pollution, etc. The argument is that non-lethal mutations which reproduce successfully (that is, adaptively to changes in immediate environment) function like sudden jumps in the progress of evolution and give rise to species variation.

However, recent work in genetics and biochemistry has shown conclusively that mutations are all but always harmful, even lethal, the cause of many physiological disorders. In any case, they could not give rise to a magnitude of change of an order to generate a new species, to make a dog a horse, or an ape a human. For such an order of change to occur randomly and then to become successfully established would require a period of time many times in excess of the highest estimate for the age of the universe.

For years, much research has been done on pigeons, dogs and flies. Though some physiological changes do occur within the same race of animals (there are different breeds of dog and pigeon, for example), such adaptive evolution *within* species is no evidence for evolution *of* species. All the extensive research done for years on Drosophila yielded nothing but Drosophila, and the research proved that Drosophila remains as it is.

Hybrid varieties are obtained by artificially crossing two species, such as horse and donkey, but the resultant hybrid (mule) is typically sterile. After long research, scientists have recognized that it is not possible to progress from one species to another. There are some insurmountable, impassable, barriers between species. That conforms to ordinary sense, as well as to the known facts and to scientific reasoning. How could such a creature as human, who has an extraordinarily sophisticated brain and is capable of (in any and every stage of civilization) of linguistic and cultural expression, of religious belief and aspiration—how could such a creature have evolved from an ape? It is quite extraordinary that even to speculate that it might be so can be given serious consideration, let alone believed and accepted as conforming to reason!

However, that acceptance of evolution is a major pillar of modern materialism, and of historical materialism in particular, as Marx and Engels insistently pointed out. It is a sort of blind faith, a prejudice, a superstition that the materialists cling to Darwinism of the crudest kind. They insist that absolutely everything be explained by material causes. As for what, by those limited means, they cannot explain, they dare not admit that they cannot explain it so. They can never allow that there must be a supra-natural, metaphysical agency that intervenes to make the biological world as it is, so wonderfully abundant, prolific, diverse and, within stable forms, so marvelously adaptive and versatile in response to local environmental possibilities.

The alternative to evolution is design which necessarily leads to the concept of a transcendent and unitary power, the Designer-Creator, God. Therein lies the reason for the continuing tyranny of the Darwinist theory: the fear that to acknowledge the Creator will bring down the edifice of an autonomous science, an autonomous human reason. An individual scientist in his or her private capacity may be a believer, a theist, but science itself must be unbelieving, atheistic. It is ironic indeed that to preserve the illusion of independent human reason, the Darwinists (and materialists generally) will defy or ignore the facts, deny and belittle logic and reason. It is to the credit of the scientific community that, in ever greater numbers, individual scientists have found the courage to question and challenge the tyranny of Darwinism in the teaching of the life sciences.

That said, it remains unfortunately true that, some young, pliable minds are vulnerable to the myth of Darwinism simply because it is the official dogma, the staple of all textbooks on the subject everywhere. How true and apt is the Turkish proverb— that a half-wit can throw a pearl into a well with ease, and forty wise men struggle in vain to get it out again. Nonetheless, there is solace in the knowledge that a lie, however mightily supported, can have but a short life. The truth of the matter is that the origin of the species, and of the major divisions of species, is not yet understood. Is it too heavy a burden on humility to say: "We marvel, but we do not know"? And we marvel most at, and understand least of all, the origin of intelligent speech, ideation, abstraction, symbolization, culture, love of beauty and variety, consciousness, altruism, morality religion, and spiritual aspiration.

To be sure, Darwin was a great and gifted scientist who must be credited with a mighty contribution to the ordering and classifying of species, and for his work on adaptation; but it should be noted that what he did well and incontrovertibly is to observe accurately and understood intelligently what was there in nature.

Whatever his own intentions, in spite of them, his work, like every reliable advance in observation and explanation, confirms the Divine Architect, the All-Mighty Power, Sustainer, Administrator, Who willed the marvelous organization, reliable, systematic, subtly integrated harmony of the operations of nature, and who combined that order with beauty. Whereas what Darwin found increases our faith in God, it led him astray.

How great, sublime, is the Creator. Order, understanding, wisdom are by His gift. Likewise, guidance to faith is absolutely in His grasp.

4.4.

What should be our attitude against ideas like positivism
and rationalism which are accepted as the sources of
information in the West? To what degree do they reflect
the truth?

Much has been said on the issue of information sources.
Some of the people who have commented on this
issue have sometimes been restricted by their knowledge and/or faith, thus they have vocalized different opinions.

According to the Islamic perspective, there are three types
of information sources:

Knowledge obtained through the five senses or relating to
these senses. These include, seeing, hearing, smelling, tasting,
and touching. For example, something that is seen is there, and
something that is felt through touching exists.

According to the trend which accepts only this source of
information, anything beyond the perception of these senses
cannot be a subject of knowledge. This positivist trend has lost
its influence over recent decades; however it was widely popular at the beginning of the twentieth century.

The second source of information is the mind. When the
"mind" is mentioned, an unbiased decision-making entity, capable of evaluating matter within its pure form, and competent of
making an objective decision is implied. The importance of a
non-degenerate, unbiased, non-oppressed, functional mind is
undeniable for information. In the modern world, rationalism is

the representative of this tendency. Since its emergence, Rationalism has always advocated the "mind" as the only source of information. However, even rationalism is not sufficient to achieve true knowledge.

Another source of information is "authentic narration." Authentic narration should be understood in two ways. Firstly, it is knowledge that has been transmitted by a number of different people and accepted as true. For example, a narration about a continent or a country to which one has never been is an authentic narration. To illustrate further, for a person who has never visited the continents of Australia or America, any accurate information, or first-hand information, obtained is of this type. It is possible that we may not have visited or seen these places, however millions of people live on these continents and hundreds of thousands of people visit these continents every year. The information gathered from these people is so powerful and trustworthy that anyone who has not seen these places cannot doubt their existence.

Secondly, authentic narration can also be considered to be that of "Divine Revelation." In other words, this would consist of the Divine Books revealed to the messengers by God Almighty, where the revelations were brought by the Archangel Gabriel.

In order to discover the wonders of the universe and to achieve a better and more accurate knowledge with our five senses and mind, we must make evaluations under the light and wisdom of Divine revelations. Only when manipulated to work under these principles will science be able to accomplish its task of producing the fruit that it should.

Human beings are not capable of seeing or hearing everything that exists, and thus they are not capable of knowing everything that exists. The mind cannot comprehend everything that exists. There are so many things that exist but which are not sensed through our senses or understood by our minds, or even, if the mind does understand them, can never be sensed or reached. Hence, the human being can only learn these facts through the teachings of a Divine Being whose knowledge, power, and will surround everything. We can only learn the things He knows to the extent that He teaches us in His Divine Books; in this way we become knowledgeable of those matters.

Otherwise, partial falsification or incorrect interpretations of the Divine Books is inevitable. Moreover, if only the senses and experience will be the basis of information, then one will be forced to say "I do not believe in anything other than what I see, hear. . ." This is tantamount to rebelling against everything that the mind puts forward. In fact, if only sensory information is taken as the basis of knowledge, then people will be forced to search for compatibility between their deduced knowledge and the universe that is created by God Almighty. In such a system, whatever facts agreed with their theorems would be true, anything else would be false. However, as God says in the Qur'an: *We did not take the human beings as witnesses to the creation of the Heavens and the Earth* (Kahf 18:51). When the Divine revelation is not taken into consideration, every explanation is no more than a theorem or a guess.

Unfortunately, because only the first two types of sources were accepted, many Divine Revelations were rejected. With the progress of science, their validity has once again been proved. For example, the stages of an embryo in the mother's womb have been well defined. When Omar Khayyam, who was an extreme rationalist, was asked about these verses, his response was to comment against the Qur'anic truth by commenting that the verses were not meant literally. Some other scholars thought that a person can only have faith in the resurrection, as it cannot be understood by the mind; however, Said Nursi has explained it with a simple analogy. The resurrection is like the spring that follows the winter. We do not have any actual sensory knowledge that this will happen, we know from observation and reasoning that the spring will come. Since some people only trust in the two types of sources, they had to twist what they read in the Divine Book, even the fundamentals of faith. For example, through the influence of philosophy, Farabi and Ibn Rushd, even though they were geniuses of their time, considered the Divine Revelations and the prophethood as being human-made concepts.

Some thought that philosophers were higher in status than the Messengers of God. The All-Knowing God was aware of how the Messengers would perform their duty of conveying the message; i.e. with an extraordinarily superior performance. This is why they were given the prophethood in advance; yet philosophers could not see this fine nuance. Moreover, it can be concluded that philosophers are only translating what Aristotle had earlier said to suit their time.

If the Islamic World is considered as a whole, it can be seen that not everybody fell into these traps. Zahrawi, Ali Kuşçu, Jalaladdin Dawwani, Gelenbevi and many others, did not fall into these traps; they were very religious, and they were very influential in their times. People like Molla Husrev and Khwarizmi, with their work in sciences that led their fields of study for many centuries, even in the West, were still able to maintain their faith without experiencing any conflict and lived for the most part as religious, pious people.

In conclusion, it would be proper to say that all sources of information must be handled together if one is to achieve an end result. Discriminating between these information sources and taking them discretely will open up pitfalls for humanity. The same pitfalls will continue to open if the same mistakes are repeated. Humanity will have to say "True" to those things it claimed as "False" the day before. However, using the Divine Revelations as the foundations of knowledge, and surrounding and framing them with the information attained from the senses and mind is the only path that will lead us in a true direction.

CHAPTER 5

Perspectives

5.1.

What are the reasons for the fact that Islam spread over such vast territories in such a short time in the past? What are the reasons for the Muslims' defeat and failure at the present time?

A Muslim could be defined as one who believes in God and the principles of faith decreed by God, who never deems the opposite of these principles even likely, and thus submits and surrenders himself to God. That is, a Muslim is one who wholeheartedly and sincerely performs and represents all His commands with respect to regulating his individual, familial and social life. However, during some periods, Muslims might have been unable to find the opportunity to represent Islam in all respects. Even so, if people burnt with the love and yearning to represent Islam and writhed in the longing to live and act upon it, God willing, they would not be responsible, blamed and reprimanded for collective failures. Any subtle, complex system dismantled and laid aside unused, its use half-forgotten with the passage of time, can only be re-assembled and made to work again after the greatest application and effort. How much more so if that system were a way of life involving the taking on of burdens and responsibilities which, in the long term productive of ease and contentment, are in the short term sometimes strenuous and arduous—how difficult to build up that way of life again, reviving the consent of not one or a few persons but of a whole society? And yet, if people are determined, persevering and sincere in the intention of making it work again, their sincerity of effort may suffice to excuse them, even though their effort did not or could not succeed. If people pursue that goal with a total commitment and yearning, as a matter of life and death, they would surely not be held accountable if the goal eludes them. In fact, in order to be exempted from the responsibility, one should either live Islam thoroughly or burn with a strong desire to live Islam and to make it a lived reality. Any acts contrary to this will entail consequences in this world and in the Hereafter. In this world, the people suffer abasement and degradation as a consequence of living apart from Islam; they will be condemned to live in all the domains of life, social, political, commercial, military, under the power and direction of unbelief, and they will be mightily surpassed in the fields of knowledge and technology. Then, in the Hereafter, they will be questioned and punished severely for all that failure, that surrender to the powers of unbelief.

For almost a thousand years, Muslims experienced civilizational rise from one level to another and earned the highest acclaim. During the period of the Rightly Guided Caliphs that rise had a sublime, heavenly quality. Those who followed the Prophet in the first Islamic century were real representatives of the true Islamic way of life. God's Messenger says concerning this period:

> Muslim armies will arrive, after me, at the gates of cities, where they will be asked, "Did anyone among you see the Prophet?" The answer will be affirmative, and the gates will be opened for them. Those who succeeded them will also perform jihad and they will be asked, "Are there any people among you who saw those who had seen the Prophet?" They will reply, "Yes," and the cities will be conquered by them. There will finally come the third generation, who will be asked, "Did anybody among you see those who had seen the followers of the Prophet's Companions?' When this question, too, receives an affirmative answer, conquest will also be bestowed upon them."[1]

Again, in another narration recorded in Bukhari and Muslim, God's Messenger says concerning those three succeeding generations: "The best of you are those who live in my period, then those who succeed them, and then those who follow them."[2]

Those three generations followed strictly in the Prophet's footsteps and, accordingly, were granted great victories.

When we look at our Islamic past, we see that the historical events confirm the sayings of the Prophet. The period of the Four Caliphs was thirty years. During the reign of the third, 'Uthman, the Muslims spread in all directions of the known world. In one direction, they went up to Lake Aral and in the opposite direction up to Erzurum in eastern Anatolia. Despite differences and disagreements at that time, the spirit of jihad against unbelief was always strong, sustaining the consciousness of being active and moving forward. During that time the Muslims conquered the northern Africa in its entirety. 'Uqba ibn Nafi' was the Muslim commander in that campaign and died at the age of 50. However, the campaign was successfully concluded within his life-time and he managed to make himself listened to and obeyed by all the Berbers. When he reached the Atlantic, he rode his horse into the sea and there stood and exclaimed: "O God! If this sea of darkness did not appear before me, I would convey Your Name, which is the source of light, to overseas lands as far as the remotest corners of the world."[3] The great Muslims of that time did not dispose of modern ships or planes that can travel in almost any weather conditions. At that time, they campaigned on a mount or on foot, and rivers were forded or crossed upon simple rafts. Despite shortage of means, the Muslims were able to travel to and conquer vast stretches of territory in different parts of the world in a remarkably short span of time.

It is one of the mysteries of destiny that wherever the Companions of the Prophet went or conquered then, there is to this day a Muslim people, even in countries far from the "heartlands" of the Arabian peninsula—such as Dagestan, Turkmenistan,

Uzbekistan, Kazakhstan. These countries still have functioning mosques and traditional religious academies, raised scholars and scientists, who were, and are still, regarded as the best in their fields, from Bukhari to Muslim, from Muslim to Tirmidhi, from Ibn Sina to al-Farabi, because Islam was lived and acted upon in those lands. We certainly believe that the splendor and excellence of an Islamic ethos, spirit and consciousness will be experienced again in those places, and the Muslims will regain their former status in the world.

That the Companions of the Prophet managed to conquer so many places in such a short time certainly has its own explanations and meaning. First of all, the Companions were wholly devoted to the cause of Islam. Superficially viewed by their enemies, they must have seemed to them to be out of their minds— certainly, their accomplishments were such as to stir and freeze all imagination. For instance, 'Ali slept in the Prophet's bed, in his place, on the night when the Prophet left for Madina and the enemies · surrounded the house intending to assisinate the Prophet with multiple sword blows. 'Ali's doing so means that he had accepted the likelihood that he would be dismembered and killed. But the polytheists' hands remained hanging in the air, so astounded were they that the person in the bed was not the Prophet but a young man who accepted such a sacrifice and thus attributed no value to the rest of his life, at the age of 17. In another instance, on hearing the continuous howls and voices of livestock and domestic animals, Abu Jahl and other polytheists climbed to the roof of the house of Abdullah ibn Jahsh to learn what was going on in there. They were struck by what they saw. All the members of the family had deserted the house to follow the Prophet, taking nothing with them, giving not a second thought, to their possessions, thinking only of moving to Madina to be with the Prophet. Upon this Abu Jahl said to 'Abbas: "How strange! That cousin of yours has caused such a split (*iftiraq*) between us that it is impossible either to explain or to understand." Home, goods and chattels, wife, children and family, and everything were left, given up, for the sake of God, His Messenger and the message he brought. How could polytheists comprehend such a thing?

While Abu Bakr was migrating from Makka to Madina, he did not take anyone along with him, but he left his children, wife and father, whom he loved dearly, back in Makka. 'Uthman did not take his wife, Ruqiyya, the beloved daughter of the Prophet, along with him while migrating. Ruqiyya was the light of the Prophet's eyes, and I certainly believe that if it were said that a life is needed for Ruqiyya, each and every Muslim would run to sacrifice his own life thousands of times for her. However, that Ruqiyya was left in Makka and 'Uthman emigrated to Madina. Such was the loyalty to the Prophet at that time.

On his return from negotiations with the Prophet 'Urwa bin Mas'ud he said the following to the people in Makka about the Companions' commitment to their cause and devotion to the Messenger of God:

> O people, I have been sent as envoy to kings—Caesar, Chosroes, and the Negus—but I have not seen a king whose men honor him as the Companions of Muhammad. If he commands anything, they almost outstrip his word in fulfilling it; when he performs his ablution, they well-nigh fight for the water thereof; when he speaks, their voices are hushed in his presence; nor will they look him full in the face, but lower their eyes in reverence for him . . .[4]

However, the Prophet advised those who stood up for him: "Do not stand up (for me) as the Persians do (stand up for their elders)."[5] As the Prophet demonstrated and lived modesty and humility, so he rose ever higher surpassing even the angels. It was narrated that when the Prophet first saw the Archangel Gabriel, he was frightened. However, as one of the saints, lovers of the Prophet, remarked: "If Gabriel had comprehended the essence of the *haqiqat al-Ahmadiyya* (the truth of Muhammad), he would have passed out and never come to himself till the Day of Reckoning." The Prophet always rose higher and higher in respect of his power of relationship, obedience, submission and servanthood to God. However, every step toward the highest deepened his humility. He presented himself as an ordinary man, one among many others, and was deeply disturbed by any other manner or treatment shown to him.

That period was such that the Companions attached themselves deeply to the Prophet and integrated with him thoroughly. When the Prophet said: "Your blood is my blood, your life is my life," the words confirmed what actually existed as a full harmony and accord. When the time came to spread and represent Islam abroad, when it was necessary to emigrate to different lands and climates, none of them asked why or what. They simply went and never thought to return to their old homes. Let alone thinking of coming back, out of the fear of blemishing the sincerity of the intention to emigrate for the sake of God only, they trembled at the thought of dying being buried in their old hometowns. Sa'd bin Abi Waqqas had fever in Makka, and was shaking with grief. When the Prophet asked the reason for his sadness, it was that he was worried that he would die in Makka after he had emigrated to Madina, and that thus his emigration would not be complete.

When marching on the Khaybar, the Prophet did not want to take 'Ali on the expedition because he had some ailment of the eyes. However, 'Ali was not willing to be left behind. He said: "Would you have me to stay behind with the women and children, O Messenger of God?" He did take part in the expedition and the citadel of Khaybar was conquered though his extraordinary courage.

Once, before leaving Madina for an expedition, the Prophet appointed Umm Maktum, a blind person, in charge during his absence. He was exempt from fighting because he was blind; the other who remained behind were women and children. Years later, when Umm Maktum learned that the Muslims were going to fight the Persians. Despite his old age, he joined the marching soldiers and expressed his wish to take part in the battle ahead.

Some Muslims, especially Mughira ibn Shu'ba, wanted him to stay away from the front, but Umm Maktum found an opportunity to talk to the commander of the Muslims, Sa'd ibn Abi Waqqas and said: "Mughira bin Shu'ba wanted to prevent me from fighting in the way of God. If any of you prevents me from fighting and dying in the way of God today, I will make complaint about you to the Caliph 'Umar." What a reason to complain about—being prevented from offering his life in the way of God! When asked what he could do, he answered: "Yes, I am blind, but this will not prevent me from holding the flag and walking straight ahead. So, I would like to hold the banner before the army." He really seized the opportunity, did not hide behind excuses, but took part in the front line, held the banner, walked forward, and found what he yearned for, martyrdom at the battle of Qadisiya.

The Companions were that kind of people, who scorned danger in the way of God, and even courted death for the sake of their true belief, and to convey it to other lands.

Though Abu Talha had grown very old, weak and feeble, when he heard that the army was preparing to go to Cyprus, he called his grandsons and told them that he would like to take part in the expedition: "I heard from the Prophet that Cyprus would be conquered[6] and I think it is time for it, and I'd like to take part in it. However, it is not possible for me to sit and ride on horse-back. Therefore, tie me tightly to the horse lest I fall off." His grandsons did not want to yield to their grandfather's wish and argued that he was quite old, and so excused and would not be accountable for being absent from the battle. However, he replied that he understood the Qur'anic verse urging people to strive in the way of God as not discriminating between young and old; he read it in the absolute sense. In the end, the grandsons were unable to dissuade him and Abu Talha joined the army in the way that he wished. However, his life did not suffice to complete the journey as he was so elderly and feeble; but he did, after all, achieve what he longed for in this world, and perhaps he might have said with his last breath: "All thanks and praise to God! You bestowed upon me what I longed for."

Another Companion, Abu Ayyub al-Ansari, who hosted the Prophet at his home, had already been married with children when the Prophet first arrived at Madina. Abu Ayyub's grandchildren helped him mount the horse before he came all the way to Istanbul (Constantinople) under the command of Yazid. From the Prophet's arrival in Madina to the rule of Mu'awiya and the command of Yazid, we may count that 40 or 50 years passed. Abu Ayyub must therefore have been around 75 or 80 years old when he arrived in the vicinity of Istanbul.

Let us pause to ask at this point: What were such Companions of the Prophet after? There are many verses in the Qur'an and there are sayings of the Prophet praising their virtues and attributes. God named them as *Ansar* (Helpers) and *Muhajirun* (Emigrants) and glorified them. They were even foretold in the Old and New Testaments (the Torah and the Gospel). They had listened to the Prophet saying that the victorious armies of Islam would arrive at the gates of Europe, and that he gave tidings that Constantinople (now Istanbul) would be conquered by Muslims. Many attempts were made to realize this and be worthy of the encouragement of these words of the Prophet: "Certainly, Constantinople will be conquered. Blessed is the commander who will conquer it, and blessed are his troops."[7]

Since that city was itself a symbol of a large dominion, the Prophet was thus directing his community to carry Islam all over the world. So the only objective they had was to be among the troops the Prophet praised and thus gain the pleasure of God. There was no other motive, ambition or purpose behind the hardships and dangers they endured. Since the Prophet pointed out the worthiness of the army in the eyes of God, the Companions were in a sense competing to become members of that army.

Hoping to be an object of the Prophet's praise, Abu Ayyub al-Ansari (Khalid bin Zayd) set forth from Madina to Istanbul even in old age. The city was besieged for weeks and months, but the Muslims were not then granted the conquest. Before that, Abu Ayyub al-Ansari was totally exhausted and waiting for death. One of the things he mostly kept asking was "Any news of the conquest?" Eventually, when the commander of the army realized that he was on the very verge of death, he asked the noble Companion of God's Messenger if he had any wish. Abu Ayyub al-Ansari said: "Take me as far as possible. If it is possible, take me and bury within the walls of Constantinople. We came to conquer Constantinople, but I see that I will not be blessed with such a conquest. On the other hand, I definitely believe that one day the tidings of the Prophet will come true and be attained by some [other Muslims]. Therefore, I would like to be buried over there. Listening to the clashing of their swords and shields in my grave will please me. Let me hear at least the voices of those blessed soldiers." Almost five or six centuries later, Istanbul was conquered by the Ottoman commander, whose name was also Muhammad (Mehmed), at the age of 22. Such sweet manifestations of destiny, as to end one period in history and start a new age, to be blessed with the tidings of God's Messenger, to break down an iron door, like the door of Khaybar, leading to Europe, to represent the Muhammadi spirit completely at his time, were the blessings bestowed on Sultan Mehmed the conqueror. He can be said to have represented the Muhammadi spirit in his time like a Mahdi; his was among the voices of the soldiers that Abu Ayyub al-Ansari wished to hear and welcome to Istanbul.

Those people who sincerely and devoutly commit themselves to either *irshad* and *tabligh* (guiding and enlightening others) or to striving by what they own (material and physical struggle, jihad with their lives and wealth) can conquer the world and hold their authority in it. As the Prophet of God expressed it in a hadith, when the fear, of death grasps the souls of the Muslims, everything gained will start to slip away piece by piece. We enjoyed great status and weight among the peoples and in the history of the world until two or three centuries ago. Now we have lost that. There can be only one explanation for this: namely, that we were victorious when we had the Islamic spirit, and kept our submission, obedience and servanthood to God in a firm and sound condition. During the period in which we started to slip backward, our souls were captured and enslaved to fear of death, and other fears, weaknesses, love for life, ambitions and concerns for our own future.

Those Muslims in the past spread to all parts of the world and conveyed the Divine Message and established the best and noblest type of rule. What can this accomplishment be attributed to other than the fact that they really devoted their physical, spiritual and material wealth to the way of God?

No matter what nation or ethnic background they were from, we see in all those heroes raised from the Islamic world the same spirit. They scorned and ignored the pleasure of living for themselves but preferred the pleasure of making others live instead. The only thing they had in mind was to spread the Religion to which they were bound as believers and followers, and they regarded that belonging as the highest honor. In the Seljuk, Ottoman or other states, in rulers like Alparslan, Kılıçarslan, Murad Hüdavendigar, Mehmed the Conqueror, Selim I, Salahaddin Ayyubi, and many others, we see the same spirit and consciousness.

Alparslan, the Seljuk Sultan, who defeated the Byzantines in 1071 and thus opened the doors of Anatolia and the vast Byzantine territories to Muslims, delivered a sermon before the Battle of Malazgirt (Manzikert), one of the great decisive battles in history, and concluded with this prayer: "O Lord, make the white clothes and robe I put on my shroud today." Those Muslims went on the battlefield to become martyrs rather than victors, and proved that with the shrouds they put on before battle. In that way they were undoubtedly ready to tackle the enemy army, often many times more numerous, without a second thought. At the end of the day, the Muslims were victorious and the enemy were defeated and captured, even the Emperor Romanus Diogenus, and we believe that Sultan Alparslan meant it sincerely when he said he was not so happy because he had not reached his goal, which was to become a martyr.

The Ottoman Sultan Murad Hudavendigar prayed throughout the night: "O Lord, make my army victorious but me a martyr" before he fought against the Serbs in Kosovo. His prayer was accepted, he defeated the Serbs, saw his army victorious but while inspecting the wounded soldiers, he was stabbed to death by a Serb. As he lay on the ground, he was asked what his last wish was. He said two words "Never dismount." Then he passed away. The wish he expressed was never to stop struggling in the way of God and carrying His Divine Message further.

The magnificent state (and states) established by people of this quality enjoyed such prestige and authority in the balance of power in the world that other nations and states looked to them and adjusted themselves and regulated their affairs accordingly. They exerted such efforts in the way of Truth, and scorned everything except that, holding God first in all plans and affairs. They thought and evaluated everything according to the Divine Will and Pleasure, and became the zealots of the Sublime Cause. For this reason God protected our borders from all intrusions, and we led a glorious and dignified life in the past. When we lost such high attributes and spirit, we were surrounded on all sides, degraded and eventually captured by our enemies. We first died in spirit and then in dignity and honor, and then in physical, material terms.

If we would like to recover and represent Islam beautifully as they did in the past, we must first recover those factors which made our ancestors attain their high rank, all of them, not neglecting a single one among them. For the truth is: . . . *man can have nothing but what he strives for* (Najm 53:39).

5.2.

What is the Islamic perspective on anticipation for the Messiah and the Mahdi?

Messiah is a name or attribute of Jesus, peace be upon him. Messiah means "blessed" in Hebrew, thus this name might have been used for him in admiration for his merits and virtues It is reported that he was given this name for several reasons: he was protected from all kinds of sins; his touch healed illnesses by God's permission; he frequently traveled and made his message heard everywhere. Mahdi literally means one who has embraced the faith and has thus been led to the "straight path." Mahdi also refers to the savior, who will come at a time when tyranny and injustice dominate all around the world; he will re-establish justice, make Islam dominant, and he will be a descendent of the Prophet (*Ahl al-Bayt*).[8]

Awaiting a savior at times when basic credo of belief is ignored, abandoning religious duties has become common, and proper conduct as enjoined by faith has been forgotten in the world, dates back very early in history. Jews, Christians, even many people before them all spent a lifetime with expectations of a savior, especially when they had to face injustice and suffer. Throughout the ages of prophetic mission that was represented by a chain of messengers, it was always a Prophet or a Messiah for whom the people waited. After the Messenger of God, people no longer await a messenger; rather they are expecting a reviver or a savior, a guide or a mahdi from the lineage of the Prophet. This mahdi has been called Mahdi al-Rasul, due to the perception that the Mahdi will be sent like a messenger by God and that there are signs of his superiority over the *Fuqaha al-Arbaa* (four great jurists of Islam: Imam Azam, Imam Malik, Imam Shafi'i, and Imam Ahmad ibn Hanbal), saints of all ranks, and even the *Qutb al-Irshad* (Master of Teachers, a title given to very exceptional saints who appear only many centuries after a previous one).

Islam and anticipation of the Mahdi

In religions like Judaism and Christianity people have always awaited a Messiah or a Mahdi, who will save the believers from sufferings and teach the faith to others. Such anticipation consolidated the believers' spiritual power and stimulated the believers' determination for revival. It can even be argued that the popularity of prophets like Moses and Jesus were, to a certain extent, a consequence of this kind of anticipation. People who gathered around each of them said, "He is the powerful will and determination that the previous messengers gave glad tidings of!" According to the New Testament (Matthew 3:11) the Prophet John (the Baptist), said, "I indeed baptize you with water unto repentance; but he that comes after me is mightier than I; he is one whose shoes I am not worthy to bear; he shall baptize you with the Holy Spirit and with fire." Although he was also a prophet, when he listened to Jesus, the most glowing youth of Nazareth, who was also his cousin, he saw his enthusiasm and influence upon people, and he said, "This is the Messiah we have been awaiting!" John's glad tidings gave rise to further enthusiasm and expectations in the community, and his testimony for Jesus quickened the process of the apostles' faith in him, reinforcing their belief.

The Children of Israel have always anticipated a Messiah. When they noticed certain features of the savior described in their holy book, their anticipation became a fire burning inside, urging them toward further research. Nevertheless, during the translations of the scriptures, or as they were handed from generation to generation, some kind of a mist covered this very important issue, making it impossible to see what was behind. Lost in this overwhelming mist, the Children of Israel became lost in their viewpoint and got mired down in denial, although the savior for whom they had been waiting was standing in front of them. They denied the Messiah who embraced everyone with forgiveness and compassion, saying, "You are not him (the Messiah)."

After Jesus another savior was awaited. The coming of the Pride of Humanity, Prophet Muhammad, was anticipated; all his attributes had been very well defined and sought after. The glad tidings of this were announced by Jesus and the messengers who came before him. Bahira, the Christian monk, expressed this longing for the coming savior when he told the following to the Messenger, who was partaking in a trade caravan to Damascus: "You will be the Last Prophet. I hope that I can live until the day when you will declare your mission, and that I will be able to serve you by carrying your shoes." Zayd (Umar's uncle, his son Said ibn Zayd was a Companion among the ten people who were promised Paradise) voiced the same anticipation when he said on his deathbed, "I know a religion will come very soon, its shade is above your heads. But I don't know if I can survive until that day."[9] However, there were also many others who failed to see the pit in front of them, denying him, saying, "You are not him." There were others who did not accept his message either because it was against their interests or because he was not of their lineage; but the glad tidings, known for so many years, that a savior would come caused the first Companions to embrace Islam and the Helpers of Madina to pledge their commitment to the Messenger of God at Aqaba. Anticipation of a Messiah had a great influence in the formation of the bond between the Prophet and his Companions, despite so many provocations and attempts to discourage the followers by the polytheists. The believers stood firm at the reverse in the Battle of Uhud and at the Battle of the Trench. In addition to the Prophet's personality, appearance, message, persuasion, confidence, devotion, loyalty, and intellect, we cannot deny the role this anticipation played in the spreading of his message.

The origins of the anticipation for the Mahdi-Messiah in religion

There are almost a hundred Traditions of the Prophet which point to the return of the Messiah at the end of time and how this return will take place. At least forty of these Traditions are authenticated according to the criteria determined in hadith studies; they are considered to be reliable by experts. Another twenty of this hundred are listed as being *hasan*, i.e., although not as certain as the authentic Traditions, their chain of transmission is considered to be dependable. Twenty to thirty other Traditions have a weaker reliability for their authenticity. To cite an example, it is reported in Bukhari, Tirmidhi, and Musnad that the Messenger of God said, "By God in Whose Hand of Power my soul is, the descent of Jesus, son of Mary, who was a just sovereign, among you, is soon. He will destroy the cross, kill the swine, revoke the capitation tax, and distribute goods in abundance. Property will be so vast that no one will accept it as charity." In another hadith, reported in Muslim and Abu Dawud, the Prophet said, "When Jesus, son of Mary, descends the ruler of the Muslims will ask him, "Come and lead the prayer for us." Jesus will say, "No, you are rulers to each other; this is a blessing of God to the Muslim community.""

There is no verse in the Qur'an that has an overt reference to this issue. However, some prominent scholars, like Kashmiri of India, who compiled Traditions related with this issue, selects four verses that are considered to indicate the descent of the Messiah toward the end of time.

> He shall speak to the people in the cradle and in manhood. And he shall be of the righteous. ('Al Imran 3:46)

And there is none of the People of the Book but will believe in him before his death (Nisa 4:159)

And peace on me on the day I was born, and on the day I die, and on the day I will be raised to life. (Maryam 19:33)

And (Jesus) shall be a Sign (for the coming of) the Hour (of Judgment). (Zukhruf 43:61)

We can also give two examples from the Traditions about the Mahdi: "The Mahdi is from us, *Ahl al-Bayt*. God will give him victory in one night. The Mahdi is from the children of Fatima."[10] "Even if there will be one day left for the end of this world, God will send a person from *Ahl Al-Bayt* to fulfill justice in a world of tyranny."[11]

As a work of His Mercy, God Almighty, at various times of disunity, has sent a restorer, a reviver, a respected vicegerent, a saint, a perfect teacher, or other mahdi-like blessed people to us. Such people have eliminated disunity, restoring and protecting the faith. Bediüzzaman gives Mahdi al-Abbasi as an example in the political arena, Abd al-Qadir Jilani, Shaykh Naqshbandi, *aqtab al-arbaa* (four great saints: Abd al-Qadir Jilani, Ahmad Badawi, Ahmad Rufai, Ibrahim Desuki), and twelve imams in the spiritual arena, saying, "As this is the way of God, He will definitely send a radiant person from *Ahl al-Bayt*, who will be the greatest jurist, the greatest reviver, sovereign, mahdi, teacher, and the greatest saint against a grievous mischief toward the end of time." Bediüzzaman also answers questions about the weakness of the reliability of Mahdi-related Traditions: "Is there anything that cannot be criticized in some way or another? Some scholars report with indignity that even Ibn al-Jawziya, a great scholar of hadith, listed some authentic hadith as fabricated. Every weak or fabricated hadith does not necessarily mean that it conveys a wrong message. A weak hadith means that its chain of transmission does not certify its authenticity; but its message might reflect the truth."[12]

The return of Jesus

Some Islamic scholars consider the descent of Jesus as a person would be contrary to the divine wisdom of God Almighty. They rather think that it will take place as a descent of a "collective spiritual personality." Some other scholars have interpreted Qur'anic verses and Traditions in a different way. Bediüzzaman, on the other hand, while not discarding the possibility of Jesus' descent as a person, stresses the spiritual personality more, and interprets this descent as the conformity of the Christian world to Islam. He also argues that the descent of Jesus as a person might not be a distant possibility: "The Glorious Sovereign, Who sends angels from heavens to the Earth at all times, Who sometimes transforms them into human form as did Gabriel into Dihya (a Companion of the Prophet), Who make the spiritual beings from the realm of spirits come to this world in the form of a man, or late saints in an imaginary body, would certainly dress Jesus in a human form who is alive and resides in the worldly sky, even if he had gone to the farthest end of the afterlife and was really dead, and would send him for such a substantial result." Bediüzzaman never went further into these details which exist in certain reports.

Claiming To Be the Mahdi Is Deviation

The Mahdi-Messiah issue is an issue that has not only long been abused, but also one that has been exploited by unbelievers who try to slander sincere believers. Some of those who make such claims are pushed to the fore by certain powers and they are used against Muslims.

I believe the descent of Messiah as a spiritual personality is not too distant a future. It may indeed take place that this spirit, or meaning, may descend, and nobody should oppose this possibility. The coming of the Messiah as a spiritual personality simply means that a spirit of compassion or a phenomenon of mercy will come to the foreground, a breeze of clemency will waft over humanity, and human beings will compromise and agree with each other. The signs of such a phenomenon are already present: Muslims are sometimes invited to churches to read the Qur'an, it is now an accepted fact that Prophet Muhammad is a Messenger of God, and that the Qur'an is a divine revelation. Some people as well may come to declare themselves as "Muslim-Christians." It does not seem improper to me to regard these as an introduction to the spirit of Messiahhood.

Abusing the Expectation of the Mahdi and the Messiah

Many individuals throughout Islamic history can be listed to have attained a rank near to that of the Mahdi. To cite an example, Mahdi of the Abbasids, may God's mercy be upon him, can be considered as a mahdi in a sense if we take into account his significant reforms, the straight path he was following, his respect for his predecessors, his reverence for the Companions, as well as his moderate and upright ideas about religious issues. Among the Umayyads, 'Umar ibn 'Abd al-'Aziz was a mahdi in this sense. It is also possible to refer to some prominent figures from Abu Hanifa to Imam Rabbani Faruq al-Sarhandi, and from him to Imam Ghazzali and Mawlana Khalid Baghdadi; for they are considered to have had the characteristics of the Mahdi. Such people served Islam sincerely, without making false claims or pursuing personal interests, and they never claimed to be the Mahdi. The people who noticed their virtues gathered around them, forming a circle of benevolence. However, there have always been some opportunists, who desired to exploit such considerations.

Even while the Messenger of God was still among us, many liars like Musaylima, Tulayha, Aswad al-Ansi, and Sajah claimed to be prophets. In addition, in every epoch some have asserted to be "the person who will come at the end of time." Similar to the people mentioned above and to the eight Dajjals who uttered that "I, too, am a prophet" soon after the death of the Messenger of God, there have been some people with sick souls in every era who state "I am the Messiah" and go even further to produce the evil claim that the Messenger of God was sent to the Arabs, while they have been sent for the world community. Moreover, it is reported in the Traditions concerning the Mahdi that the Prophet said "Someone from my family will appear and his name will be similar to my own"[13]; that is, it has been indicated that the Mahdi's name will be similar to the names of the Prophet, for example, Muhammad or Ahmad; a number of people have changed their names to fit in with this fact.

According to what was reported by Shatibi for instance, Abu Mansur, the ruler of the sect called Mansuriya, honored himself with the name "Kisf," which literally means "piece," claiming to be the Messiah and that the Holy verse *"Were they to see a piece of the sky falling (on them), they would (only) say: 'Clouds gathered in heaps!'"* is referring to himself (Tur 52:44). Indicating this passage and claiming that he was the *kisf* he soon gathered supporters around him, as if he had indeed descended from Heaven. Ignoring the actual meaning of the verse, and only taking into account the action of descending from the sky, he argued to be the *kisf* mentioned in this verse thinking of himself as a stone that had descended upon humanity. Similarly to what Shatibi reported, Ubaydullah of the Rafizis, who thought of himself as the Mahdi, had two councilors, Nasrullah and Fath. Nasrullah in Arabic means the "help of God," while Fath means "victory." As if to justify his status, this so-called Mahdi assured them with the argument that "You are the ones the chapter Nasr in the book of God refers to; as the verse surely addresses us, the promise that Islam will be embraced by people in crowds will come true via our own efforts":

> When comes the Help of God, and Victory, and you see the People enter God's Religion in crowds, celebrate the Praises of your Lord, and pray for His Forgiveness: For He is All-Forgiving." (Nasr 110:1-3)

These two examples, reported by a man of significance like Shatibi, are sufficient in terms of providing evidence for how names and attributes can be abused, how they are used in the service of disorder, and how they cause bloodshed in a particular geographical area.

The issue of awaiting a savior and the abuse of this expectation has not remained restricted only to religious life. Some people, for instance, awaited a savior in economical terms while others did so in a social context. Those who awaited a savior for economy focused their attention upon Karl Marx during a chaotic time of Europe which was mired in blood by the uprising of workers. Such people have highly regarded his works *Das Kapital* and *The Communist Manifesto* which he wrote with Engels, and thus regarding him as the savior of humanity, and in particular, the working-class (the proletariat). Dr. Ikbal stated the following words about Marx in *Payam Mashrik* (News from the East): "a prophet without a holy book (!), who is voicing the people's viewpoint"; he further depicts Marx as an ignorant, impolite, and impious character who is after various kinds of expectations; and this Marx was indeed greeted by some as the Messiah. Likewise, from Lenin to Trotsky, many others have been applauded as saviors. At times in the Islamic world, too, some have been viewed as saviors in nearly every country: from Egypt to the Sudan and from Syria to Somalia. Some have even gone to such an extreme in apostasy, ignorance, heedlessness and unbelief that they even said, "Muhammad was the Prophet of the Arabs, or Madina; yet, this one is ours."

Several mahdis emerged among the followers of the Rafizi thought throughout history. Similar to the argument that the person who founded the Muwahhideen State was the Mahdi, many political groups that emerged during the times of the Umayyads and Abbasids were convinced that their leaders were Mahdis. The first sovereign of the Shiite (Ismaili) Fatimid State, which was established in North Africa and exercised power over Egypt later on, was believed to be the Mahdi by those who founded and sustained this state. Placing a child on the throne, they would gather around this pseudo-savior whom they considered to be the grandson of the Prophet, thus abusing the Mahdi—Messiah issue.

Furthermore, the Fatimids declared independence causing further disorder as well as segregation in the Muslim community during a phase in which the Muslims suffered at the hands of both the Crusaders and the Mongols.

As for recent history, it is as if the Mahdi-Messiah issue has provided a playground in which disorder can frolic. It has been abused to a great extent by a number of people, from the Mahdi of Somali to the great Mahdi in Sudan; the latter was killed and cremated by the English and his ashes were then scattered on the Nile—Dr. Ikbal wrote a great deal about this matter. There is also Bahaullah, who was applauded as the Promised Messiah, and Gulam Ahmad, who was engaged in Hindu yoga and meditation, having a tendency toward revealing the power of the soul and seeing hallucinations when he felt dizzy, due to his asceticism. This last person called himself respectively a *mujaddid* (reviver of religion), the Promised Mahdi, the Expected Imam, and finally the Promised Messiah. Later came Elijah Muhammad, who declared himself to be a prophet.

A particular case in point is the Shiites' attempt to keep the idea of the Mahdi on their agenda by announcing that "One of the Twelve Imams has been hidden somewhere while still alive, so as to be able to appear at a later date." It is very ironic that they expect the savior who kept cover from the evil of the Abbasids will suddenly make his appearance as if from behind the Mountain Qaf,[14] during the time of the Dajjal (Anti-Christ), which is a much greater evil than was present under the rule of the Abbasids. This expectation should be investigated in terms of the essentials of faith as well.

The expectation of a perfect Heracles has always been an everlasting characteristic of the oppressed and victimized nations. Many lazy, passive, and weak souls, who have completely sealed themselves to abolishing false beliefs through their own efforts, are busy awaiting such a Heracles who is to descend from the sky. As a matter of fact, there exists such a reality and there is a tendency to await a Mahdi in Sunni thought as well; however, the

Mahdi, as understood by the Ahl al-Sunna, has not been attributed supernatural features at all. On the contrary, he is believed to be a ruler who will lead the society to Islam, and a man of science, heart, and spirit.

It Is Necessary To Watch Out for Abuses

Having been subject to abuses throughout the history, the belief in the Messiah and Mahdi might still be open to exploitation, while liars who claim to be prophets as well as imitators of the Mahdi and so-called shaykhs may well spring up. If a person can claim to be the Messiah, as Gulam Ahmad did, it is, then, necessary to study and analyze the issue in terms of the essentials of faith. What does he mean by such a claim? If he is trying to say that the Messiah has entered into him, as have some people attributed divinity to Jesus, and that he regards himself in this way, this is unbelief according to Muslim faith; the word "deviation" is too mild a term for such a situation. Yes, such a claim is blatant unbelief.

By this utterance and claim such a person may mean to say that he is on a spiritual journey in the orbit of Jesus the Messiah, and that those who observe him are able, in some way, to see a (kind of) Messiahhood through him, due to the level he has attained. If this is what is meant, it is a paradox, as a person who has actually reached that level would never make such a claim. In addition, claiming to be a person of such a spiritual rank is the height of vanity.

Abd al-Qadr al-Jilani may have really been a Mahdi, though he had never claimed such a thing. Likewise, Muhammad Bahauddin Naqshbandi might also have been a genuine Mahdi; yet, he had never associated himself with that rank. Though he equally deserves to be addressed as Mahdi in this sense, Imam Rabbani did not even consider himself to merit the quality of being human. To speak more frankly, those who belong to the horizon mentioned above are surely the ones who avoid claims and quests for high spiritual rank and status.

Perfect analysis is required for such claims: Is it a wrong association arising from sharing the same level of spirituality?[15] Is it an error which stems from an overestimation by society? Is it the voicing of the confusion of that same society? Or is it rather that this person truly thinks that he is a chosen one? If they really believe so and claim to be the Mahdi, then this is an obvious sign of vanity, deviation, and a groundless claim that should be refuted. If, in the same way, they argue that they are the Messiah, then this is nothing less than the worst kind of unbelief. Nobody can claim "I am the Messiah," as Jesus the Messiah came, and took his leave of us, going as prophet. This being the case, anyone who claims to be the Messiah is without a doubt performing an action that is as grave as claiming to be a prophet, that is, they are blaspheming. If a person born of certain parents claims to be the Messiah, it means that they have been reincarnated as well, an idea that finds no place in Islamic belief, where such a claim is regarded as a deviation, or even unbelief. From this perspective, one would never attempt such an argument if following the way of Ahl al-Sunna and walking in the light of the Prophet.

As I have mentioned earlier, Bediüzzaman Said Nursi put forth the idea that If there is a need for Islam, the manifest religion, to express itself in various places in the world again, the Messiah will come back right away, even from the remotest corner of the other world. However, in order to shed light upon his general outlook, he interpreted the descent of Jesus as a spiritual personality. He further stated that the Messiah would be represented by a group or a section of the society. Yet, in this context, giving a particular name, or perceiving the personality of Jesus epitomized in another person, or declaring that a specific person is the Messiah, be he the great Conqueror Mehmed II, or Imam Rabbani, are all in essence unbelief. It is an evil claim that genuine believers are afraid to utter; rather they are on constant alert to avoid it.

Some naïve people might easily call those whom they overestimate as "the Mahdi." As we have tried to emphasize, however, even if the Messiah were to come and descend in person, he would not do so as a prophet. The fact that he will obey the current guide of Muslims in addition to the fact that the Messenger of God, Muhammad, was the last prophet, both indicate that he will neither descend as a prophet nor will his spirit pass into another. If he were to appear as spiritual personality, neither those involved in this spiritual personality nor the leading figure would never come up with such a claim. Similarly, the person in question, or rather the spiritual personality, who bears the attributes of the Mahdi, would not claim to be the Mahdi nor would they ever make such an assertion. Thus, even if they do not believe themselves to be the Messiah, if a person remains silent against the overestimation of others regarding him who proclaim him the Messiah or the Mahdi, this means that he is keeping silent against deviation or unbelief, depending on the gravity of the claim. Accordingly, such a person would deserve more to be called "a mute devil," based on the statements of God's Messenger.[16] Indeed, if one is addressed as "the Messiah" but, on the other hand, remains silent purposefully, not attempting to warn others against making this deviation, then such a person is no less than a mute devil. If the person in question wanders around claiming that "I am the Mahdi," they indeed float on misery, and have gravely deviated from the path. It is out of the question that a Muslim would approve of any such claims.

This issue, which was destined to be abused throughout time, has unfortunately become a tool exploited by the enemies of the religion, used to defame sincere believers. Moreover, some other people are backed by certain powers to emerge with such claims to use against Muslims. Such cases may well come to the fore in the near or distant future, just as they did in the distant and recent past. In Turkey, people who have deviated, as well as those who do not believe at all, the ignorant with diplomas, and representatives of violence who rule over the fate of the Turkish nation or Muslim nations around the world might well take advantage of the expectation of the Mahdi-Messiah and exploit the meaning of such a title on behalf of their plots. This will be done in the name of deceiving Muslims through the exploitation of Islamic concepts and by condemn sincere Muslims to annihilation. This is a particular danger during the current phase in which Muslims around the world are suffering under oppression; the masses are depressed. Therefore, it is of the utmost importance that care and caution be adopted against such plots and against the exploitation of such concepts.

5.3.

How are those who are hostile to dialogue activities today relevant to "Kharijites, Karmatis, Anarchists"?

Karmatism is a heretical esoteric sect founded by Hamdan ibn Karmat in the ninth century AD. Hamdan took advantage of the poverty of people and was influential, especially in Iraq and its periphery, voicing "collective property" and claiming shares from the rich. These people may have appeared religious on the outside, however, they had an economic theory, political zeal and objectives. They attempted to rebel against the Abbasid caliphate, gathering forces around them, and they tortured Muslims of the Sunni path for years, martyring many. They ambushed pilgrims on their way to the Hajj, attacked the sacred city of Makka, and they even stole the Hajar al-Aswad from the Ka'ba and took it to Basra.

Not accepting marriage as an institution, Karmatis named forbidden acts as being "fine arts." They treated women as collective property and led the youth astray through prostitution, the legitimization of drinking wine and alcoholic drinks, and made every kind of indulgence lawful. In short, enslaved by their carnal desires and aspirations the Karmatis designed a religion of their own; they labeled anyone who did not follow their way as being "hell-bound," and thus managed to fabricate disunity for a long time. In one sense, they can be seen to be the anarchists or nihilists of their time.

Modern Kharijites

The Kharijites were another heterodox faction which blamed Caliph 'Ali, first for conceding to arbitration and accepting the treaty at the Battle of Siffin and second for not handing over the caliphate to Muawiya and thus being guilty of a "grievous sin." They declared all others who did not think likewise—including the Companions of the Prophet—infidels. Although they apparently believed in Islam, their vision was narrow and deprived of sound thinking. Action always took precedence over knowledge and learning for them; they were subsequently dragged into bigotry, hostility, and intolerance, getting mired in harshness, violence, and crudity. They were distracted by their slogans and action, which they had turned into a religion shaped by their rioting and restless character. They were motivated, not by knowledge, but by slogans, enthusiasm, and reactionary mood. Perhaps they read the Qur'an time after time, but it was a literal reading and they always opposed any interpretation other than theirs. They regarded those who thought otherwise as infidels whom were to be obliterated; they were cruel and tyrannical without a single drop of mercy.

Today, we have seen some people who behave like modern Karmatis and Kharijites, obstructing endeavors for dialogue and understanding, disrupting the dreams of peace and friendship. They too call themselves Muslims; yet, they have attacked the religion from some esoteric approach, replacing it instead with their own passions and thrills. Some others, entrapped in bigotry, have construed the literal meaning of the Qur'an and the hadith as the only primary essentials, sharpening their blades of hatred and hostility against other Muslims. A subgroup within them has adopted a deep esoteric understanding, considering themselves as having attained a transcendental existence, and look down on other Muslims. Still others, however, have blindly adhered to overt divine commandments (*nass*) with no effort whatsoever to use their mind to interpret them. They have been deprived of any proper techniques of teaching faith or of understanding others; they have no code of conduct, good morals, or respect. What all of these people have done was to start the fire of disunity and to fan the movement of tolerance.

These two groups were later joined by a third: anarchist souls. The Karmati zeal and the Kharijite restlessness pushed some Muslims into the web of terrorists, causing them to be involved with chaos, threatening and even murdering people. Whatever the motive was, be it national or religious, some imprudent individuals were manipulated by some dark power sources. They were denied the slightest share of religion by their actions; yet they committed murders on behalf of it, and handed over their trump card to those who were already standing opposed to religion.

Anarchists, Murderers of Innocents!

Anarchists legitimized the actions of some tyrants against Muslims. They came into being as rebels against the state, and they refused to recognize democracy or the secular system. The natural outcome of such a situation was that the state used it as an excuse to suppress such insurgences. In the meantime, obscure suspicions were construed as actual incidents and many innocent people were hurt on the false grounds that "there is a possibility that they may be dangerous." In Islam there are no suicide bombers. All throughout history Islam has never issued permission to murder innocent people; this is out of the question. However, as a consequence of the actions of some people, people similar to the Karmati and Kharijites, who have been deceived or manipulated by drugs or in some other way, many other innocents have been defamed, and pristine image of Islam has been tarnished. Muslims, the representatives of submission to God and security, have been depicted as potential terrorists.

Two factors can be listed which aggravate the issue: the first is the fury, coercion, and determination of the tyrants; the second is the actions and conduct of some imprudent people which substantiate the cause of the tyrants.

Throughout the process, the greatest harmed have been those in the middle, those in doubt and hesitation. They have observed what has been going on, and seeing in the front those anarchist souls, nihilists, and a few Karmatis and Kharijites, they thought "they have done far too much, they deserve punishment." In this way, they have endorsed the coercive operations of the tyrants, perceiving them as being carried out in defense of the system. Moreover, those in the administration either then deliberately overlooked all that was happening, or were incapable of comprehending the true extent of things. Those people who hesitated in the middle were overwhelmed by their doubts and consented to the deterioration of the atmosphere of tolerance and to the hands that had been extended for peace being pulled back.

It is also important to note that it is always easier to inflict damage; damage can be influential, even if it is apparently small in size or carried out by only a few. Destruction is easy. Libeling, lying, slandering can always be done very easily by a few hired writers. Many people, as well as many institutions, have been defamed in this way. They have even organized slander campaigns concealed by the so-called "freedom of press." These campaigns were always brought to a court of law to be refuted and compensated; however, these trials lasted months and a verdict was reached at a much later date. The evil intentions had already been fulfilled, leaving behind tainted images in some minds.

A small marginal minority which was unsatisfied with everything was behind all this wickedness. They believed in a kind of caste system in which they formed the eyes, ears, nose, and mouth of Divine Existence, whereas the rest of the people were made the fingernails, or in the words of the poet Necip Fazil, they were simply pariahs. If something good were to take place, it was surely accomplished only by them; if any achievement were made, it was certainly them who were to be associated with it. How is it possible that religious people are first to be remembered when dialogue and tolerance are mentioned? How can it be that Muslims are in the forefront of education? This is not possible, it should be these others who are being appreciated for these activities, as they form the eyes and ears, not those whose essence is fingernail. You may call them a marginal group or an oligarchic minority, these arrogant people damaged extensively the peaceful aura that could have surrounded us; what they did was destructive.

Attacking Dialogue

Karmati zeal, Kharijite thought, and the anarchist mood have been seen in the past, and they can reappear at any time. As long as people of faith can recover and have an opportunity to express themselves, take a stand in favor of dialogue and understanding, voice peace everywhere and to everyone, surely there will be some others who will be disturbed by them. Perhaps we should ask them this question: "People of faith act upon certain principles and their numbers constantly grow as they are welcomed by everyone; why don't you use your own arguments of unbelief so that you may grow in number too? You are not appreciated by the society. You have to reach such a level that you are countable, inspire confidence, and become beloved so that you may be welcomed."

I would prefer not to have mentioned these three groups of evil people, especially as we are experiencing the blissful month of Ramadan. The mention of evil blockades mercy; thus, talking about these people breathing evil may prevent the divine mercy pouring down upon us these days. To ensure that these blessings are continued perhaps we should always speak about the good-doers and take action for the good. I was inspired by the recent fast-breaking dinners of representatives of many different thoughts dedicated to tolerance, each holding each other's hand, exchanging glances; no more are their looks of "the other." I wish some people had not sabotaged such activities in the past, that they did not take on hostility and could embrace these gatherings with good intentions; I wish they could at least respond to those hands extended for peace, by holding out an olive branch.

Everyone shows their true character. We are also supposed to continue showing our true character. Our path is that on which we are inspired with faith in God and on which we take positive action. Our duty is to invite others for "conversations about the Beloved for another hour," as the Companions would do, and in that way to reinforce our faith and to enthusiastically walk, making the truths of belief accessible to others; it does not matter what some other people say or do.

5.4.

How would you describe the moral transformation of the Prophet's Companions after the advent of Islam?

The Messenger of God lived in an age that well-manner had been long forgotten and in a place in which daughters were subject to infanticide. You will have an idea of their well-manner, by only looking at the way they spoke. At that time of the history, a child called his father by name; like "'Umar", like "Abu Bakr" and his mother like "Umm Salama." Once a bedouin asked questions to the Prophet one after another about obligations of a believer and then as if in a negotiation said, "By God who sends you down, I will not perform neither more nor less than this." Someone named Dhu'l-Khuwaysira, while dividing the shares, came to the Prophet and said, "Be just, O Muhammad" in an inappropriate manner. Let's suppose that manner was toward ourselves; well, it is possible we could be unjust. However, the one who was being addressed in this inappropriate manner was the Prophet who was under the protection of God. He, on the other hand, absorbed all of these rude acts and language. Why? Because it is the most important task to help someone earn the eternal bliss and he was facing every cruelty in order for his community to reach the salvation, the eternal bliss.

Among people like these, came out the Companions of the Prophet who are a miracle of the Qur'an because the Qur'an led them to the morality step by step with these verses below:

> O You who believe! Do not put yourselves forward before God
> and His Messenger; but fear God, for God is He Who hears
> and knows all things. O you who believe! Do not raise your
> voices above the voice of the Prophet, nor speak aloud to him
> in talk, as you may speak aloud to one another, lest your deeds
> become vain and you do not perceive. (Hujurat 49:1-2)

The phrase in the first verse: "Do not put yourselves forward
before God and His Messenger" means, when a question asked
or if there a problem occurred in the presence of the Prophet, do
not jump to answer or solve the matter for God will let His consent known through the Prophet; and following his footsteps is
to obey God's rules. Therefore, do not attempt to teach the
Prophet how he will answer by getting into the conversation
before him. Therefore, well-manner toward the prophets is well-
manner toward God since they open our way to the eternal bliss
by bringing down the revelation and by illuminating it with their
teachings.

When the second verse "Raise not your voices above the
voice of the Prophet" was revealed, Thabit ibn Qays ibn Shammas
went home and started crying out that he was doomed to
Hellfire. The Prophet asked his neighbor, Sa'd bin Muadh about
Thabit. He went to see how he was doing. Thabit said, "When I
heard this verse I thought that I will be one of the residents of the
Hellfire because I have the highest pitched voice." Then Sa'd narrated the situation to the Prophet. The Prophet called him and
said that he indeed will be among the residents of Heaven. Sa'd
had a very high pitched voice by nature so the Prophet told him
that it was his natural voice and what was meant in this verse was
he who spoke in an inappropriate manner in a very rude way.

Educated and disciplined by the Qur'an, the Companions
have captured the degree of perfection in well-manner. They
became the examples for the future generations. Nobody raised
their voices in the presence of the Prophet any more and everybody spoke and acted in a very well-mannered way. Nobody
among them spoke before his turn, accorded his voice before

speaking and tried to finish their question or comment the shortest way possible. They were aware that any rude behavior toward the Prophet would cancel all of the good deeds they had performed. And a time came that their well-manner toward him reached to a degree in which like they had a bird on top of their head and in order to make that bird not to fly away, they were afraid of moving a muscle. So they were that quite. They set the examples for us by not wasting any of words of the Prophet in their life.

NOTES

CHAPTER I
WISDOM IN THE MESSAGE OF THE QUR'AN

1   Bukhari, *Iman*, 37; Muslim, *Iman*, 1.
2   Hakim, *Mustadrak*, 2/437; Tabari, *Tafsir*, 19/22; Bayhaki, *Sunan al-Kubra*, 3/363.
3   Bukhari, *Manaqib al-Ansar*, 51, tafsir al-sura (3) 6; Ibn Khuzayma, *Sahih*, 1/116; Hakim, *Mustadrak*, 3/548; Ibn Hibban, *Sahih*, 16/441-442.
4   Muslim, *Zuhd*, 10; *Musnad*, 4/168.
5   Bukhari, *Manaqib* 22; Muslim, *Fadail al-Sahaba*, 100.
6   Ibn Sa'd, *Tabaqat*, 2/121.
7   Muslim, *Jihad and Siyar* 58, Ibn Kathir, *Tafsir*, 3/560-561.
8   Tabarani, *Mu'jam al-Awsat*, 6/250; Baykhaki, *Shuab al-Iman*, 1/136.
9   Abu Dawud, 2/53; Muslim, 5/170.

CHAPTER 2
ETHICS AND SPIRITUALITY

1   Muslim, *Birr*, 43
2   Bukhari, *Riqaq*, 38
3   Muslim, Tawba, 29-30

CHAPTER 3
VIRTUES AND HARDSHIPS IN THE SERVICE OF ISLAM

1   Nursi, Bediüzzaman Said, *Sunuhat-Tuluat*, 36.
2   Tirmidhi, *Fitan* 73; Ahmad ibn Hanbal, *Musnad*, 2/390.
3   Tabarani, *Mu'jam al-Kabir*, 10/173; Hakim, *Mustadrak*, 4/349.
4   Ibid.
5   Bukhari, *Hajj*, 1, *Sayd* 24; Muslim, *Hajj*, 407.
6   For more about *tahajjud* see: Tirmidhi, *Mawaqit al-Salat*, 51; Abu Dawud, *Salat*, 49; Ibn Maja, *Masajid* 14.
7   For the hadiths stating that God forgives His servants' sins through the five daily prayers see: Bukhari, *Mawaqit*, 6; Muslim, *Masajid*, 282; Tirmidhi, *Amthal*, 5; Nasai, *Salat*, 7; Imam Malik, *Muwatta*, safar, 91.
8   For the hadith stating that a servant is made closer to God through supererogatory prayers, see: Bukhari, *Riqaq*, 38; *Musnad*, 6/256.
9   See Baqara 2:22, Naba 78:6.
10 Taha 20:53; Zukhruf 43:10-14.
11 Anbiya 21:32.
12 Nursi, Bediüzzaman Said, *The Flashes Collection*, 26th Flash, Sözler, Istanbul: 2000.
13 Ibn Hisham, *Sirat al-Nabawiya*, 2/285.
14 Bukhari, *Maghazi*, 79; Muslim, *Tawba*, 53.
15 Imam Malik, *Muwatta*, Qadar, 3.
16 Nursi, Bediüzzaman Said, *The Letters*, Seeds of Truth, 32nd epigram, The Light, Inc., New Jersey: 1998.

17 Bukhari, *'Ilm*, 45, *Jihad*, 15; Muslim, *Imara*, 149-151; Abu Dawud, *Jihad*, 26.
18 Hakim, *Mustadrak*, 4/342; Tabarani, *el-Mu'jam al-Kabir*, 8/140; Darakutni, Sunan, 1/51.
19 Bukhari, *Tafsir al-Sura*, 3; Hakim, *Mustadrak*, 2/326.
20 Nisa 4:125.
21 Bukhari, *Anbiya*, 19, *Manaqib*, 13; Ahmad ibn Hanbal, Musnad, 2/96, 331.
22 Bukhari, *Fada'il al-Ashab*, 5; Abu Dawud, Adab, 9.
23 Zumar, 39:2, 11.
24 Bukhari, *Ahkam* 5, 6, *Ayman*, 1; Muslim, *Imara*, 13, 16, 17; Abu Dawud, *Imara*, 2; Tirmidhi, *Nudhur*, 5; Musnad, 5/173.
25 Bukhari, *Iman* 37; Muslim, *Iman* 1, 5, 7; Abu Dawud, *Sunan*, sunna, 16.
26 Tabari, *Tarikh al-Umam wa'l-Muluk*, 4/250-252; Yaqubi, *Tarikh*, 2/126-127.
27 Ibn Sa'd, *Tabaqat*, 3/306-307; Mas'udi, *Muruj al-dhahab*, 2/303.
28 Muslim, *Fadail*, 59; Ahmad ibn Hanbal, *Musnad*, 6/465; Ibn Hajar, *Isaba*, 2/187; Ali al-Muttaqi, *Kanz al-'Ummal*, 10/505; Ibn Hisham, *Sirat al-Nabawiya*, 4/137.
29 Ibn Abi Shayba, *Musannaf*, 7/276; Munawi, *Fayd al-Qadr*, 3/278.
30 Muslim, *Imara*, 133; Tirmidhi, *'Ilm*, 14; Abu Dawud, *Adab*, 115.
31 Bukhari , *Adhan*, 8; Abu Dawud, *Salat*, 38.
32 Bukhari, *Tafsir al-Sura*, (17) 5, *Tayammum*, 1; Muslim, *Iman*, 326-327, *Masajid*, 3

CHAPTER 4
SCIENTIFIC ISSUES

1 Bukhari, *Tib*, 19; Musnad, 2/443.
2 Muslim, *Iman*, 249, *Fitan*, 118; Tirmidhi, *Tafsir*, 6; Musnad, 2/201, 491.
3 Bukhari, *Tib*, 1; Ibn Maja, *Tib*, 1.
4 Abu Dawud, *Tib* 1; Tirmidhi, *Tib*, 2, 5; Ibn Maja, *Tib* 1; Muslim, *Salam*, 88-89; Ibn Maja, *Tib*, 6.
5 See Ibn 'Abd al-Barr, *Isti'ab*, 4/1711; Ibn Kathir, *Bidaya wa al-Nihaya*, 7/90-91; Ibn Athir, *Kamil fi al-Tarikh*, 2/560.

CHAPTER 5
PERSPECTIVES

1 Bukhari, *Fada'il al-Ashab*, 1; Muslim, *Fada'il al-Ashab*, 208-9.
2 Bukhari, *Fada'il al-Ashab*, 1; Muslim, *Fada'il al-Ashab*, 212.
3 Ibn al-Athir, *Kamil fi al-Tarikh*, 4/106.
4 Bukhari 3:180; Ibn Hanbal 4:324; Tabari 3:75
5 Abu Dawud, *Adab*, 151-152; Ibn Hanbal, *Musnad*, 5:253
6 Ibn Kathir, *Al-Bidaya wa l-nihaya*, 7, 152.
7 Another narration of the hadith is as follows: "Certainly, Costantinople will be conquered. How good is the commander who will conquer it, and how good is his army." Ahmad Ibn Hanbal, *Musnad*, 4/335; Hakim, *Mustadrak*, 4/422.
8 Abu Dawud, *Mahdi*, 4, 5; Ahmad ibn Hanbal, *Musnad*, 1/99.
9 Ibn Sa'd, *Tabaqat al-Kubra*, 1/162; Tabari, *Tarikh al-Umam wa'l-Muluk*, 1/529.
10 Ibn Maja, Fitan, 34; Darimi, Mahdi, 1
11 Ahmad ibn Hanbal, *Musnad*, 2/117-118.

12 Nursi, Bediüzzaman Said, *The Letters*, 19th Letter, 4th Sign, The Light, Inc., New Jersey: 1998.
13 Tirmidhi, *Fitan*, 52; Abu Dawud, *Mahdi*, 4; Ahmad ibn Hanbal, *Musnad*, 1/376, 377, 420.
14 Islamic theology acknowledges the existence of this mountain called Qaf, however, there is no recorded information about its nature. Bediüzzaman briefly explains in his *Muhakemat* (First Article, 12th Introduction, 3rd Issue) that the horizon itself might be this mountain as it is believed that the world is surrounded by this mountain. He further asserts that it might be a mountain that will appear in the Hereafter, but its foundations are in this world. It is used in eastern tales to denote unreachable distances, impossible missions, and mysterious destinations.
15 Here we can give the example Khidr, who is a beloved servant of God and an important figure in Sufism. He holds a high spiritual rank and those who reach this rank through spiritual journeying are sometimes confused with the Khidr himself (for further reading, see Nursi, S., *The Letters*, Kaynak, Izmir: 1998)
16 Ibn Qayyim, Jawziya, Jawab al-Kafi, p. 69, 113; Nawawi, *Sharh al-Sahih al-Muslim*, 2/20.

INDEX